SOLFERINO 21

Solferino 21

Warfare, Civilians and Humanitarians in the Twenty-First Century

HUGO SLIM

in association with

Norwegian **Red Cross**   **BritishRedCross**

German Red Cross   ICRC

HURST & COMPANY, LONDON

First published in the United Kingdom in 2022 by
C. Hurst & Co. (Publishers) Ltd.,
New Wing, Somerset House, Strand, London, WC2R 1LA
© Hugo Slim, 2022
All rights reserved.

Distributed in the United States, Canada and Latin America by
Oxford University Press, 198 Madison Avenue, New York, NY
10016, United States of America.

The right of Hugo Slim to be identified
as the author of this publication is asserted by him in accordance
with the Copyright, Designs and Patents Act, 1988.

A Cataloguing-in-Publication data record for this book
is available from the British Library.

ISBN: 9781787386839

www.hurstpublishers.com

Printed in Great Britain by Bell and Bain Ltd, Glasgow

For Asma

'is it not a matter of urgency, since unhappily we cannot always avoid wars, to press forward in a human and truly civilized spirit the attempt to prevent, or at least to alleviate, the horrors of war?'

– Henri Dunant, *A Memory of Solferino*, 1862

Contents

PART THREE
HUMANITARIANS

Note on the Text

This book reflects the author's views alone and does not necessarily represent the positions of the members of the advisory group or the organizations that they represent.

Foreword

The story of Henry Dunant's experiences on the battlefield of Solferino back in 1859 launched the International Red Cross and Red Crescent Movement and defined a method and philosophy on humanitarian action. The book, *A Memory of Solferino*, has been translated into many languages and continues to provide inspiration to millions across the globe as they endeavour to make a difference to the lives of people affected by armed conflict. The very simple but compelling idea of reducing suffering during war has stood the test of time. How this is done today is another story.

It was against such a background that this book, *Solferino 21*, was envisaged. It was conceptualized as an opportunity to stop and reflect upon the changes that have washed across the battlefield landscape and beyond in the last 160 years—provoking ideas and views on how to address the future of humanitarian action. It does not aim to update such a pioneering text as Dunant's, nor to re-visit the visions and reflections expressed by him so many years ago. Rather, the author takes us on a journey of change, highlighting a range of new 'tipping points' and providing us with the big issues linked with war, civilians and humanitarians.

Hugo Slim was well placed to undertake such a task—from his elegant previous writings, teachings and research on this theme to the range of roles he has played in humanitarian organizations over many years. The spread of COVID-19 rendered impossible his initial intention of walking across conflict sites and imagining what different experiences Henry Dunant may have encountered. The book is, therefore, focused more on observations and new perspectives. However, the opportunity it provides for the reader to delve into considerations of the major challenges facing humanity in the area of war and the humanitarian response in the twenty-first century has in no way been diminished.

This work, which was undertaken by the author at the Oxford Institute for Ethics, Law and Armed Conflict, was supported by the British, German and Norwegian Red Cross societies as well as the International Committee of the Red Cross. As individuals drawn from each of these institutions and organizations, but acting in our personal capacities, we were privileged to serve as a group of advisers for this exciting project. We had something of a front-row seat through the different phases in which this book was conceived and the main lines of argument developed, and during which the text began to take shape. Our task was to provide reflections and feedback over the course of a series of meetings. From our respective vantage points as humanitarians or scholars, we very much appreciated the opportunity to get a bird's-eye view of the state of war in the twenty-first century.

While there are many works that provide details and analysis of specific aspects of war and of humanitarian action, this book provides an opportunity to see and assess a number of key developments at the same time. The reader is able to stand back, to view the trend lines and to get a sense of what it is that defines and shapes war and the humanitarian response to it in this century. As the author points out, just as the main features of war were about to change when Dunant wrote his book, so we seem to be on the cusp of new changes today. In addition to taking the reader through the changes that are about to come, the book explores the most significant changes of the recent past. Present and future technological developments are perhaps the most obvious changes to analyse and reflect upon, and this book provides an overview of where we seem to be going in this regard.

However, some of the most important changes to the experience of war have not just been in relation to 'hardware'—weapons and physical things—but relate to ideas and our view of morality. As the author points out, today the civilian—and not the combatant—stands at the centre of attention with regard to war. Her experience—and it is most notably the female experience—captures the attention in a way that would not have been imagined, either when Dunant wrote or even in the middle of the twentieth century. As the book explains, while civilian deaths unfortunately continue to be a central and tragic aspect of war, the overriding civilian experience of war in the twenty-first century is about the deprivations that war brings. That experience is most often one of lack of access to food, water, shelter and safety, and the displacement that so often comes with conflict. Sadly, many of these deprivations are not just a side effect of war but, rather, a tactic by belligerent forces.

This book explores how humanitarian agencies have responded and should respond to the civilian experience in war. Here again, the author argues that not only have there been significant changes, but there should, in his view, be further changes. There should be a rebalancing between the international and national character of the humanitarian response. He calls for greater localization and decentralization of humanitarian action. While not all will share his views about what the right prescriptions are, and whilst also we as individuals did not share the same opinion, there remains much useful and nourishing food for thought in these pages. The important matters raised in this book will be part of the ongoing debates by humanitarian workers globally and locally, decision makers, funders, scholars, and perhaps even donors.

We hope furthermore that this work will help inspire yet another generation of humanitarians. By bringing the focus from the past to the future, it not only takes the reader through that journey, but also provides ample inspiration and substance for anyone wishing to join the tribe of humanitarians. For them the history, principles and application of normative frameworks visited in this work will become a guiding star.

Advisory group of members from the British Red Cross, the German Red Cross, the Norwegian Red Cross, and the International Committee of the Red Cross

September 2021

List of Abbreviations

A2/AD	area access and access denial
AAP	accountability to affected people
ACLED	Armed Conflict Location and Event Data Project
AMA	artificial moral agents
AI	artificial intelligence
ASEAN	Association of Southeast Asian Nations
ATT	Arms Trade Treaty
B2B	business to business
B2C	business to customer
C2	command and control
CAR	Central African Republic
CBO	community-based organization
CHS	Core Humanitarian Standard
CoH	conduct of hostilities
DAC	Development Assistance Committee of the OECD
DRC	Democratic Republic of Congo
ECOSOC	Economic and Social Council (UN)

FAO	Food and Agricultural Organisation (UN)
GBV	gender-based violence
HCI	human–computer interaction
HDX	Humanitarian Data Exchange
HEA	Household Economy Approach
HGM	hypersonic glide missiles
IAC	international armed conflicts
IASC	Inter-Agency Standing Committee
ICC	International Criminal Court
ICRC	International Committee of the Red Cross
IDMC	Internal Displacement Monitoring Centre
IDP	internally displaced person
IED	improvised explosive devices
IFI	international finance institution
IFRC	International Federation of Red Cross and Red Crescent Societies
IHL	International Humanitarian Law
IHRL	International Human Rights Law
INGO	international non-governmental organization
IoT	Internet of Things
IPV	intimate partner violence
IRC	International Rescue Committee
ISg	Islamic State group
ISIS	Islamic State of Iraq and Syria
LGBT	lesbian, gay, bisexual and transgender

LGBTQ+	lesbian, gay, bisexual, transgender and queer/questioning and others
M2M	machine-to-machine communication
MDH	misinformation, disinformation and hate speech
MSF	Médecins Sans Frontières
NATO	North Atlantic Treaty Organization
NGO	non-governmental organizations
NIAC	non-international armed conflicts
NTS	non-traditional security
OCHA	United Nations Office for the Coordination of Humanitarian Affairs
OECD	Organisation of Economic Cooperation and Development
OTH	over the horizon
PMC	private military company
PNSP	Productive Safety Net Programme
PoC	protection of civilians
PRIO	Peace Research Institute Oslo
PSEA	prevention of sexual exploitation and abuse
RoE	rules of engagement
RPG	rocket-propelled grenade
SPACE	social protection approaches to COVID-19 (British government)
UHC	universal health coverage

UNHCR	United Nations High Commissioner for Refugees
UNICEF	United Nations Children's Fund (originally United Nations International Children's Emergency Fund)
UNRWA	United Nations Relief and Works Agency
WEOG	Western European and Others Group (UN)
WFP	World Food Programme (UN)
WHO	World Health Organization (UN)

Introduction

This book is about war and humanitarian aid in the twenty-first century. It looks at the story so far, what we might expect in the next ten years, and how we should prepare for it. I was prompted to write it when re-reading *A Memory of Solferino* by Henry Dunant in June 2019, the 160th anniversary of the great Battle of Solferino in northern Italy in 1859.[1] This was the great battle where Dunant had his idea to create the Red Cross. Dunant's short book, which describes the battle and his humanitarian efforts to protect the wounded afterwards, is the founding text of the Red Cross and Red Crescent Movement. Part memoir and part policy paper, it made an urgent humanitarian call for change when it was first published in 1862 and had astonishing results. Dunant's powerful book helped to launch a global humanitarian movement and an international law to protect the wounded in war—the First Geneva Convention in 1864.

Shortly after the 2019 anniversary, several of us in the Red Cross and Red Crescent Movement agreed it might be useful for someone to examine the state of war and humanitarian response 160 years after the Battle of

Solferino, in a similar spirit to Dunant but with a twenty-first-century view. I was invited to try, and I was funded for a year by the International Committee of the Red Cross (ICRC) and the Red Cross Societies of Britain, Norway and Germany to produce a book of similar structure and length to Dunant's. My task was threefold: to gauge how far the world of war and humanitarianism has come since 1859; to use Dunant's book as a prompt to analyse twenty-first-century war and humanitarian response to date; and to look ten years ahead. This book is the result and I hope it fits the bill. I have called it *Solferino 21* to encourage humanitarians to look at twenty-first-century war and humanitarian aid with the same innovative gaze that Dunant brought to them in the nineteenth century.

For everyone in the Red Cross and Red Crescent Movement around the world, Dunant's memoir functions as an almost sacred text. Its account of human suffering in war and its determined humanitarian vision remind them of the battlefield origins of the Red Cross and Red Crescent and affirm their movement's enduring humanitarian insight that war's cruelty and suffering must always be countered by a practical spirit of humanity, an internationally respected system of humanitarian law, and well-organized compassion.

Dunant started his book by recounting the 'horrors' of the Battle of Solferino, which marked a turning point in the Italian War of Independence. He then described his own voluntary humanitarian work and that of many others, as they helped thousands of wounded soldiers in the days immediately after the battle. It was in Castiglione, a village near Solferino, where Dunant, a devout Swiss businessman, saw a need to set up the Red Cross and organize an international treaty to protect the wounded in war. Surrounded by the sight, sound and smell of disease and death, Dunant experienced the human consequences of war and had his big idea.

Dunant joined military medics, priests and hundreds of volunteer women from towns and villages all over northern Italy to try and ease the suffering of military men whose bodies were torn apart by bullet, blade and blast. Several soldiers died in front of him from gangrene's fevered and agonizing death. Many were beyond help from the medicine of the day: their jaw blown away, their nose sliced off, their deep abdominal wounds infected with maggots. Dunant joined in to bring them food and water, dress their wounds, write letters home for them, and comfort them as they died.

Dunant was there as 'a mere tourist'. He was trying to arrange a business meeting with the French Emperor to present him with a zany political tract he had written, which exhorted Louis-Napoleon to become a global Christian emperor and reconquer the Holy Land. That book rightly failed, and Dunant's humanitarian experience made him write a better book and launch a movement that ranks every human life as equal and valuable. If Dunant was an accidental humanitarian, the hundreds of Italian volunteers he worked alongside were there very deliberately to help the wounded of both sides in a war they cared about deeply, being eager to have their own independent country at last. Once wounded, the despised Austrian occupiers and the heroic Italian nationalists and their powerful French allies were recognized by ministering Italian women as *tutti fratelli*—all brothers— and equally worthy of care.

This kind of humanitarian work for the wounded and sick in war was not unusual. For millennia before Solferino, women and men of goodwill, like these Italians, had cared for the wounded after the countless battles, raids, skirmishes and sieges that constitute the bloody history of war. As I write, thousands of people are doing the same today in wars around the world, described as 'first responders' in modern humanitarian jargon. Dunant's great contribution was to foresee how humanitarian help could be formalized in a new organization, with humanitarian rules internationally agreed in law. Like any good Swiss, he was shocked at the apparent disorganization all around him after Solferino and by the fact that there was no proper system of relief that ticked along precisely, like a Genevan clock. True to the sexism of his age, Dunant was also appalled that 'so many weak and ignorant women' were in charge and that there were not enough 'kindly and capable men on hand' to grip the problem firmly and take command.

In fact, of course, the system was not as shambolic as Dunant saw it. As always in a crisis, the situation was initially overwhelming, as all around him 'every church, convent, house, public square, court, street, or pathway in these villages was turned into a temporary hospital' (p. 35). There was a basic but very inadequate system of military medical posts, which flew black flags, and, in a few days, a system of triage was up and running which moved wounded soldiers by wagon and train to hospitals in major cities like Brescia and Milan. Here, wealthy ladies and gentlemen had self-organized, like their village counterparts, to fund and procure medical supplies and set up a large network of families to meet wounded soldiers off the trains and care for them in their homes after treatment. Dunant describes how the wounded arrived in Milan 'at the rate of one thousand a night... Every family which had a carriage came to fetch wounded men from the station' (p. 53). This practice of hosting the victims of war, which we see in many places like Lebanon, Jordan and Nigeria today, was integral to national humanitarian action in the Italian War of Independence, too.

Dunant's account describes this impressive national humanitarian network at the same time as he expresses his Swiss anguish at its apparent untidiness. His conviction that it could be improved was right, and Dunant's humanitarian vision was more national than international. He dreamed of national humanitarian networks taking centre stage and being supported by the expertise of an international relief society, with work for the wounded protected by international law. Dunant's priority was the professionalization of national networks of relief societies that would shoulder the critical mass of response, with an international organization playing a smaller, enabling and gap-filling role.

Re-reading Dunant's powerful and rhetorical text 160 years after his experience of war, three things jumped out at me: pivotal moments in warfare; the significance of civilians; and the importance of national humanitarian systems. These three themes will be the focus of this book and are summarized here so you know what is coming.

A Pivotal Moment in Warfare

The first thing to strike me was that warfare stood at a pivotal moment of technological change in 1859, just as it does in 2021. The Battle of Solferino was a traditional nineteenth-century military confrontation fought in an old-school way shortly before warfare changed dramatically in scale and method. In 1859, military power was on the point of being revolutionized in a new era of industrial warfare and a new arms race from the 1860s onwards. The warfare that Dunant described was about to enter an era of trains, telephones, automated weapons, tanks and planes that would be unimaginable to the men who fought and died on 24 June 1859. Today our world is in another technological revolution and a new arms race, from industrial war to computerized war.

Dunant's creation of the Red Cross and Red Crescent Movement and the new treaty to protect the wounded in war came just in time before the age of industrialized war. The Battle of Solferino signalled the end of one era in warfare and the beginning of a new one. It was the last European battle in which two reigning monarchs commanded their armies in the field. It was similarly old school in that it was fought across a single battlefield in a single day, taking a prompt fourteen hours. Some 300,000 men—a huge number compared to today's battles—fought it out with rifles and artillery, although much of the fighting was still hand-to-hand, with killing done by blade and rifle butt as well as by bombshell and bullet. The Austrians lost 14,000 people killed and 800 missing. The French and Italians suffered 15,000 killed and 2,000 missing. Although terrible, these figures and the nature of the fighting were similar to the great pitched battles of the Napoleonic Wars earlier in the century. In these ways, Solferino was archaic. But its improved armaments and the railways that moved and supplied the French army pointed the way to the new era. Five years earlier, in the Crimean War, the British had used the electric telegraph for the first time in war, passing messages in the new Morse Code and opening the era of modern military communications.

Just two years after Solferino, in 1861, the American Civil War mobilized American society in a total war that used ferocious levels of artillery and ship-to-shore bombardment alongside the first modern repeater rifles and the multi-barrelled Gatling gun. In 1884, Hiram Maxim 'improved' on this in London by inventing his Maxim machine gun, which fired 600 rounds a minute and was used by British, French, German, Italian and American colonialists to massacre African, Asian and Native American forces. In 1898 at the Battle of Omdurman in Sudan, the British used these weapons and new hollow-point Dum Dum bullets in industrial killing that almost exterminated a Sudanese army in a morning, killing 12,000 Sudanese and wounding 13,000, with a loss of 47 British troops killed and 382 wounded. Poison gas entered the military repertoire in World War I and was later used by the Italians in Ethiopia and by Nazi Germany to murder millions of Jewish civilians in the Holocaust during World War II. Warfare also took to the air at scale alongside mass mobilization and huge new artillery weapons on land and sea. This all produced industrial levels of killing, wounding and destruction, in twentieth-century battles that lasted round the clock across huge fronts for weeks and months at a time, and that were no longer fought in a day. From 1945 onwards, nuclear bombs tragically marked the peak of industrial war.

Today, in 2021, the world stands at another 'Solferino moment' as the age of industrialized warfare passes into the new era of computerized warfare, and expands beyond land, sea and air into outer space, cyber space and information space. The tipping point at Solferino was perfectly symbolized by the industrial railway supplying the front for the first time while two emperors on horseback commanded their forces in the field for the last time. Today's military shift is equally well illustrated by a simultaneity of new and old in which drones and computer-guided weapons attack a majority of soldiers in Africa and Asia who are still reliant on rifles and explosives but with mobile phones in their pockets that are linked to satellites in outer space. The drones and the phones are a sign of the highly computerized warfare that is to come, while the rifles and improvised explosive devices (IEDs) of the industrialized age are still doing most of the killing.

Computerized warfare's digital technology, with its increasing automation, extension to outer space and expansion of artificial intelligence (AI), puts the military world at a new critical juncture. Warfare is changing again. And it is changing in an era of climate crisis, urbanization, space travel, virtual living and increasing infectious disease that will inevitably transform the geography and environment in which wars are fought. This will demand comparably large changes in the regulation of war and in the humanitarian organizations that ameliorate human suffering during war—just as it did from the 1860s onwards.

The Significance of Civilians

The second thing to strike me was the absence of civilians in Dunant's account when they are so central to war today. The term 'civilian' emerged a hundred years ago in the 1920s when political and humanitarian attention turned to 'non-combatant suffering' because it reached such huge proportions during and after World War I. Although it was caricatured as a war of largely military suffering in the muddy trenches of Europe, 7 million civilians are estimated to have died across Europe and the Ottoman Empire in West Asia.[2] Civilian suffering also extended into Africa, South Asia and China, from where millions of men in particular were transferred as soldiers and labourers, leaving many women to run impoverished households on their own. In all areas of World War I, civilians endured displacement, deprivation, family separation, starvation and disease, and were subjected to extensive atrocities if they were Armenian or Belgian.[3]

Today, war is all about civilians when before it was about soldiers. Dunant described war through a very narrow frame—as a military and medical phenomenon, an activity of armies, battle, male bodies, wounds and hospitals. The military drama of war has always mesmerized the human imagination. But the military aspect is just one dimension of war, and a relatively small one today. Above all, war is a socio-economic phenomenon and usually a widespread socio-economic catastrophe. Today, the violence of war coerces large sections of society into destitution in places like Syria, Yemen and Nigeria, destroying their assets, their families, their livelihoods, their markets, their public services, their future plans and their life chances.

Most people experience war as poverty not as battle, and the civilian has rightly taken the place of the wounded soldier as the lead character in the humanitarian account of war today. Dunant was not in war for long. His short experience meant he focused on wounded soldiers in front of him and not on the civilian suffering around him. Local Italians were not trapped and attacked on Solferino's large battlefield, as civilians are in Syria today, but their farms and fields were certainly destroyed, their stores, homes, possessions, sons and daughters requisitioned. People were displaced, impoverished and raped across large parts of Italy as three major armies moved around and clashed repeatedly. Dunant saw glimpses of this and made some reference to it. But civilian experience was not seen and valued then as it is now.

In 2021, Dunant's humanitarian heirs look at war primarily through civilian eyes. It is the civilian, not the wounded soldier, who stands in the centre of the moral frame we put around war. This change has occurred for several reasons, some military and some political. Military medicine has improved greatly since Solferino. Since 1945 most soldiers have been ensured good preventive medicine to stop them dying of disease, and they are routinely prioritized and cared for today by their own armed forces with help from Dunant's descendants in the ICRC and Médecins Sans Frontières (MSF).[4] Better military healthcare has combined with smaller wars to bring about a consistent decline in the death and injury of soldiers. Most wars since 1945 have been militarily small wars with fewer military combatants, and casualties usually in the thousands rather than hundreds of thousands.

Civilian suffering has also become morally visible, politically recognized and better understood since Dunant's time. In no small part, this is thanks to Herbert Hoover, the American Dunant, who worked miracles for European civilians in and after World War I by organizing food relief that reached 100 million people, thereby inventing modern war relief. But Hoover's industrial-scale relief operations in occupied Belgium and across post-war Europe were building on a major political change—the age of democratization. This gave many civilians the vote and made them a political constituency in their own right, whose support began to count in the winning of a war. Total war also gave civilians strategic war work in manufacturing, food supply and the production of morale, making them a key part of the fight.

One other aspect of international society's moral evolution has played its part in putting civilians centre stage in war: the gradual (and still incomplete) moral rejection of slavery, misogyny, massacre and genocide has begun to draw clear lines about the kind of violence that is acceptable in human society, even if people seldom fight within these lines when war begins. Civilian massacre, enslavement and rape were once customary in war. Today they are morally and legally challenged.

These political trends ensured that civilians became integral to war and so attracted both attack and defence, protection and abuse. Civilians have always been hurt, starved, dispossessed, killed and raped in war, and profoundly impoverished by it. But, from World War I onwards, their suffering has become increasingly controversial and is no longer regarded as peripheral, unfortunate and inevitable. These ethical and political trends mean civilians now *have* a stake in war as citizens with rights, whereas before they *were* a stake in war as the chattels of great lords, to be murdered, sold, exchanged, enslaved or sexually abused at will.

Early twenty-first-century humanitarianism is marked by the extraordinary level of attention it has given to civilians, whose many rights, needs and vulnerabilities are now understood in terms of gender, ability, age, ethnicity and class; and whether they live in urban, rural, pastoralist, physical or virtual space. Humanitarian recognition of civilian needs has extended far beyond the food, water, medical care, shelter and family contact of Dunant's humanitarian encounter. Civilian needs today include civil and political protection, jobs, digital connectivity, livelihoods, financial inclusion in the banking sector, education, recovery from sexual violence, mental health, mobile communications, identity documents, data protection, family reunification, return, resettlement and land rights after displacement, and the right to co-design, participate and complain in relief programmes. One might say that today's humanitarians are obsessed with civilians and with every detail of civilian lives. They are ambitious to repair civilians' socio-economic wounds as expertly as today's war surgeons are able to repair the physical wounds of Dunant's beloved soldiers.

In truth, most of today's humanitarian operations, with their majority focus on food security, cash and livelihoods, are more the legacy of Hoover than Dunant. But, if twenty-first-century warfare becomes a Great Power contest once again, we can expect to see very high levels of military casualties in new big wars. The militarily small wars of the last thirty years have tended to hurt civilians more than soldiers. In Great Power military confrontations, which may be on their way, we should be ready again for massive numbers of combined civilian and military casualties, and for many more prisoners of war who may, in the future, even be dispatched to another planet for safekeeping.

The Importance of National Humanitarian Systems

The third thing to jump out at me from Dunant's memoir and to resonate with humanitarian discussions today is his emphasis on the need for more investment in national humanitarian networks. This sits at the heart of his vision. This century, humanitarian aid has been more concerned with internationalizing its norms and organizations. Dunant dearly wanted both. But his vision from Solferino has been reversed as international organizations have come to dominate humanitarian aid in wars around the world, often treating national networks as inferior amateurs prone to political bias. Indeed, Dunant did this himself while also urging their professionalization. Because he could not immediately recognize his own type of orderly system in the frantic activity going on around him, he mistook it for a failing system. Yet, his own account simultaneously shows that there was, in fact, a rather amazing humanitarian system coming into being under enormous pressure and with a distinct northern Italian cultural feel.

Alongside his genuine humanitarian insight, Dunant's cultural and sexist bias began a humanitarian superiority complex that has travelled down the years and is still evident today. This sense of superiority has created an imperial form of humanitarian aid that is marked by strong elements of Western paternalism and maternalism, which dictate more than they enable as they rightly seek to help. Professor Michael Barnett describes today's international humanitarian system as 'an empire of humanity'.[5] We have, in the West at least, gone the other way to Dunant's nationalizing vision and created international superagencies which stride the world and dominate the money, space and discourse of humanitarian aid. This was not the balance desired by Dunant.

The COVID pandemic of the last couple of years shows us how it is totally normal for nations of all kinds to stumble at first or in the middle of an overwhelming crisis, as they gradually find a way to build a humanitarian response of their own. Some, like China, Korea, Vietnam, Liberia, Sierra Leone, Senegal, Australia and New Zealand, who have previous experience with similar pandemics, acted fast and well early on. Others, like the UK, USA, India and South Africa, have erred and stumbled but are emerging with their own systems, experience and expertise, which would surely never have developed if China and Korea had simply flown in, taken control and deployed their own systems and staff. National self-determination is an important part of building lasting and culturally adapted humanitarian capacity, and it is not respected as much as it should be today by overbearing and imperial international humanitarians. Western international dominance in humanitarian aid needs to change as we head for a new era of warfare and humanitarian response in an equally new world of Great Powers and intensifying climate crisis.

Dunant's instinct to invest equally in national humanitarian networks is fairer and wiser. When many countries are simultaneously battling climate crisis, unplanned urbanization, conflict, displacement and disease, it is best to invest in single national humanitarian systems that can cope with such concurrent and compound crises in people's lives. A parallel system of international intervenors setting their own rules and operating their own national humanitarian platforms is destructive and diluting of national capacity.

Current calls to 'de-colonize' humanitarian aid make good moral and political sense if they lead to high-performing national networks that still encourage international norms, humanitarian solidarity and practical cooperation on transnational problems like war, climate, migration and health. The commitment to invest in national networks must always remain the main operational focus of humanitarian aid and the first objective of international response. Anything else is probably colonialism of a kind that creates new problems of its own. National networks will also produce problems of their own, but then, at least, their societies will need to own them. Under imperial humanitarianism, aid-recipient governments too often deflect national problems and blame them on interfering outsiders.

Today's international humanitarianism has also embraced Dunant's non-political view of war and looks upon national networks with a suspicion of their political bias. Dunant's political agnosticism is one of his most enduring humanitarian legacies. His account of Solferino recognizes the nobility and bravery of the men who fought it. He has an evident affection for them as honourable people trying to win a 'glorious victory' and acquit themselves well in battle to make their comrades and their regiments proud. But, in his mind, it is the 'horror of war' that counts most, a phrase he uses repeatedly and rhetorically. For Dunant, war's reasons, its justifiable moral purpose and its victories are rendered null and void in the blood-drenched mud of the battlefield and the agonizing deaths of young men. He was not interested in why people fight for things like self-defence, liberation, justice, domination and greed. His account of the Italian War of Independence is morally myopic and disinterested in political right and wrong or the wider justice of a war. The humanitarian gaze exemplified by Dunant focuses only on war's cruelty and the potential for greater civility in an inevitable but misguided human activity. But this is only one way of seeing war. War's suffering can also be regarded as essential, morally important and virtuous in a just cause.[6]

Dunant's politically agnostic frame, which he crafted into a universal narrative, has cascaded through humanitarian organizations since he wrote, and twenty-first-century humanitarians have made a strong recommitment to neutrality. The humanitarianism of UN agencies, Western governments and many international non-governmental organizations (INGOs) prioritizes political neutrality and independence from warring parties. This prevents the life-saving work of many people and organizations who take sides in war from being fully recognized as 'humanitarian'. They are often excluded from direct Western humanitarian funding and heavily controlled as sub-contractors by 'real' international humanitarians.

If today's non-political humanitarian orthodoxy were applied at Castiglione in 1859, it is quite likely that the Italian villagers and grand ladies in Milan and Brescia would have been denied funding by the humanitarian departments of Western governments and UN agencies because their neutrality and independence were suspect and they were deemed too personally involved in the conflict. Instead, ICRC, NRC and MSF would have been funded to take over in Castiglione and Milan because they would have been politically agnostic about Italian independence and properly 'principled'. The duchesses and princesses in Milan, and the village women in Castiglione, would have been hired as local staff and excluded from executive meetings and decision-making. Such unfair political screening happens in many conflicts today.

If Dunant were to return to earth, presumably from heaven, and visit the war zones of the 2020s, I expect he too would wonder about these three big challenges facing humanitarians today. He would feel a pressing need to understand the dramatic changes in warfare and want to set humanitarian limits to new methods and weapons of war. I think he would be surprised that it is now the civilian who holds the moral centre of gravity in humanitarian aid and he would be pleased at how many governments and agencies are attending to their needs. He would stand amazed that every person in war has human rights, and he would be impressed by the hundreds of pages of new Geneva

Conventions and International Humanitarian Law (IHL) agreed by states. Such progress—ethical, legal and operational—would surely gladden Dunant just as much as the new arms race, the climate crisis and the high levels of human suffering in war would alarm him. Just as he worried in 1859 about the capacity of national relief societies to cope with the suffering of people in their own lands, I expect he would be delighted to see how global the Red Cross and Red Crescent Movement has become in its 192 national societies, their federation and the ICRC. But I also think he would regret that, all too often, national humanitarian systems are marginalized, under-resourced and wrongly playing second fiddle to much larger international superagencies.

This Book and Its Author

Sadly, this book was written at a distance. My original plan was to walk around some of today's battle spaces, as Dunant had done around Solferino, to observe war and humanitarian action at first hand. The COVID pandemic and its long periods of lockdown have prevented this and I have had to be content to look on today's war and humanitarian action from afar. I ask forgiveness for any of the book's shortcomings that result from my inability to see war and humanitarian aid close-up this year. Nevertheless, I hope the observations that follow still offer a useful perspective on war and humanitarian response as it is happening in the twenty-first century and as it may develop in the next ten years.

I feel the reader should know something of the person they are reading. I am a white British man, educated in the classical European tradition, and with a degree in theology and a PhD in humanitarian studies. I have spent my professional life between international aid agencies large and small, and universities old and new. As a humanitarian, I worked in famines near the frontlines of civil wars many years ago in the 1980s and early 1990s and have visited countries at war on and off since then. I have also worked in humanitarian policy and diplomacy in Geneva and around the world for several years. In academia, I have led a Master's programme for humanitarian workers for ten years and worked as a researcher and visiting professor for several years. I have never been bombed, shot at, displaced or imprisoned in a war, but I have seen people suffer terribly and die because of war and listened to many people in Africa and Asia talk about their experience of war. As a child, I grew up in a military family surrounded by kind soldiers and war veterans. I also have talented women and a number of priests in my family background. This mixture of good soldiers, spiritual priests and intelligent women is probably why I have lived my life in thrall to the better integration of war and kindness, a puzzle I have tried to resolve in a humanitarian career.

What follows is in three parts, like a triptych with three painted panels. Each part can be read as an essay on its own. Part One looks at war's political, military, technological and legal dimensions to see why and how warfare has been made in the twenty-first century, and how it is likely to be made in future. I explore the political reasons for war today, and ten main characteristics I see in warfare so far this century. I then look ahead to the risks of a return to 'big war', pressing ethical questions around AI-based computerized warfare, and war in an era of climate crisis and disease.

Part Two is about war as a socio-economic disaster, which has such a deep impact on millions of civilians who are forced to make new lives from its violence and destruction. I examine what we know about how civilians suffer and survive. I criticize how humanitarians sometimes misrepresent civilians' experience of war, especially around gender and scale, and discuss the remarkable survival and agency of most civilians. I then think ahead about how civilians will experience future warfare amidst other global megatrends and in their new virtual lives as digital civilians.

Part Three is about humanitarians. I look at the largely Western system of international humanitarian response, its major innovations this century and some of the challenges it will face in the next ten years. In particular, I examine the national–international question, known as 'localization' in humanitarian policy, and insist that we must find a better balance between global and local in humanitarian aid in time for the pressing demands of climate emergency and big war.

Before you start, please remember that this is not a definitive work on war and humanitarian response in the early twenty-first century. It simply describes some of the key features as I see them, prompted by Dunant's famous book. Nevertheless, I hope it will be a useful text for humanitarians, military professionals, diplomats and students, and even for civilians who are living through war as they read it.

Part One

WARFARE

War is very much alive in the twenty-first century, just as it was in Dunant's time. In the first twenty years of this century, there have been wars in 54 of the world's 193 countries, and most of these wars are still continuing today. Around 60 states and 100 armed groups were actively making war in 2020, according to the ICRC, with many other states supporting these wars in principle and practice as diplomatic, financial and arms-trading allies. After a dip in conflict towards the end of the 1990s, the number of wars began to increase again from 2012, alongside a renewed prospect of war between Great Powers, like China, Russia, India, the USA and Europe.

1

Warfare So Far This Century

Our century so far has not been an age of big wars. Early twenty-first-century warfare has caused terrible suffering but has, so far, been militarily small. Its casualty rate, both combatant and civilian, has also been relatively low. The twentieth century saw a series of militarily large wars. These involved mass mobilization and huge clashes between Great Powers, which killed many millions of combatants and civilians, and caused extreme suffering, destitution, impoverishment and heartbreak to many millions more. Enormous industrial wars were fought out between empires. Old empires were defeated and new states were made all over the world. The short period between 1911 and 1919 was an extraordinary historical moment that saw the end of five empires in just eight years: the Chinese, Ottoman, Hapsburg, Russian and Hohenzollern Empires, four of which had been the political bedrock of their regions for hundreds of years. World War II then saw challenges to French, British, American and Soviet power from aspiring new imperialists in Japan, Nazi Germany and Italy. The end of this war saw the USA and the Soviet Union stand supreme as superpowers. In 1949, after four decades of civil war, China's resurgence as a Great Power resumed under the Chinese Communist Party.

The so-called Cold War that followed between the Soviet Union, the Western alliance and occasionally China between 1945 and 1989 involved many hot and extremely violent wars across Asia, Africa and Latin America. Between 1945 and 1999, an estimated 3.3 million people were violently killed in 25 inter-state wars and 16.2 million people in 127 civil wars,[1] most famously in Greece, Indonesia, Korea, Vietnam, Malaysia, Bangladesh, Algeria, Nigeria, Ethiopia, Somalia, Angola, Mozambique, Sudan, El Salvador, Nicaragua, Honduras and Guatemala. Many of these wars were fought as insurgency and counter-insurgency as colonized peoples fought for independence, or competing factions fought it out to secure their new states for communism, capitalism or their own ethnic group, often in vicious proxy wars sponsored and supplied by the USA and the Soviet Union. Post-Ottoman Arab states attempted to uproot their rival Israel and secure a Palestinian state in several wars, while Turkey and Iraq fought civil wars against their Kurdish minorities, Yemen fought itself, and Iran and Iraq went to war against each other. India, Pakistan and China clashed with one another at different times, and Sri Lanka saw a long civil war around the rights of its Tamil minority.

In 1989 the Soviet Union collapsed and new wars emerged across the Balkans, in former Yugoslavia and the Caucasus, in Georgia, Chechnya, Armenia and Azerbaijan. The end of the Soviet Empire produced new states and resuscitated old ones. Afghanistan continued in conflict from its Cold War power play, and many African countries—like Somalia, Rwanda, Zaire (now the Democratic Republic of Congo), Liberia and Sierra Leone—fought new civil wars once they were released from the sponsorship of the USA, the Soviet Union or their colonial rulers. A brief period of US global hegemony in a so-called 'unipolar' world saw rare consensus in the United Nations Security Council from 1991 and states began to go to war under UN mandate, so that the UN itself became a belligerent. Throughout the 1990s, the Council deployed hundreds of thousands of blue-helmeted UN troops and UN-mandated forces in major expansions of peacekeeping and military intervention of various kinds, which tried to protect civilians and resolve civil wars in states in which no major powers had a significant interest.

It is important to summarize the twentieth century's history of imperial war, Cold War, civil war and UN war for three reasons. First, because it forms the backdrop to the history of war in our own century and shows how early twenty-first-century war has not yet been fought on the same scale as twentieth-century war. Second, it warns us that this could easily change because Great Power competition is reasserting itself today as imperial-sized powers like the USA, China, Europe, Russia and India explicitly confront each other once again. Third, humanitarians today need reminding about twentieth-century wars because they are prone to claim that wars today are unprecedented in their horror. A particular verbal trick in current humanitarian rhetoric, voiced repeatedly in media and fundraising appeals, is to say that people are suffering in war 'more than ever'. This is not true. In fact, although it feels blasphemous to say so in front of Afghans, Syrians, Yemenis, Congolese, Nigerians, Ethiopians and many more, war in the twenty-first century has not yet been as horrendous in scale and intensity as war in the twentieth century when industrial warfare reached its peak. Humanitarian response is also much better today than it was in the twentieth century. But it is still early days, and we are entering a new arms race at a time when war retains a firm grip on politicians and civilizations across the world.

War's Continuing Grip

War remains extremely resilient as a political strategy that is actively planned or pursued by governments and armed groups. War is also a pervasive feature of human behaviour that is daily imagined by billions of people in gaming, films and stories, while it is lived out for real in blood, explosions, displacement and rape by millions of others. As such, war has a firm hold on the human imagination and on national and global politics, and will continue to shape political change, government budgets, businesses, technology, the entertainment industry and human experience throughout the 2100s. Great Powers and billions of ordinary people still believe in war. They put their faith in its organized violence as a means to deter their enemies, ensure their survival and influence the world in their own best interests. Although most of us dread war, and even despise it and wish it did not exist, many of us also admire it and think it may be necessary. Most people prefer that their country has an army, and pacifism remains a minority view. Only Costa Rica and several very small states have no military forces today.

The world's Great Powers have enormous armed forces, which they are constantly preparing and upgrading for war. The USA, China, Russia and many middle powers are constantly evolving their military technology and skills in readiness to fight in three new domains beyond land, sea and air: outer space; cyberspace and information space. Between them, the USA, China and Russia spent $1,100 billion on military and defence in 2020. This spending is 7.9% of the US annual budget, 4.7% of China's and 11.4% of Russian government expenditure. The arms industry is big business.

Even if states are not fighting each other as much as they did in the twentieth century, they are making it clear that they are ready to do so. War remains a policy of last resort for states, ostensibly at least, and is illegal under the Charter of the United Nations except in self-defence or as an enforcement operation agreed by the UN Security Council to 'maintain international peace and security'. Nevertheless, states prepare for war intensely and continue to practise it widely, even if they seldom 'declare war' these days.

Hundreds of non-state armed groups have also decided that violence suits their purposes in the twenty-first century and have taken up arms to bring about their goals. They, too, believe in war and deploy it as a central policy to deliver their political ambitions by fighting with and against states, and each other, in most of today's wars. Like British government policy, these armed groups also support 'the utility of the military instrument', even if they might not describe their conviction in such delicate and bureaucratic terms.

All this shows that war is very obviously a central policy of twenty-first-century governments and armed groups, even if they both often frame it as defence. Explicit in their determination to defend their territory or their values is a commitment to make war. Nor is war an unreasonable policy for states and armed groups, depending on the threats they face.

What Is War?

I am using the word war as if we all know what it means and could easily describe it. We can, of course, but it is still useful to define it politically and legally. At its simplest, war is politically recognizable as a set of four ingredients:

- politically motivated organized violence against one or more opponents termed formally as 'enemies'
- the suspension of the normal moral and legal ban on killing, injury and destruction, and the development of the science and skills to do these things deliberately, expertly and at scale
- a process of rapid social change that typically creates widespread death, destitution, poverty, destruction, innovation and reorganization
- a certain legitimacy as a practice of states and rebels with laws to guide its conduct

Until recently, we might also have described warfare as the primary preserve of men but, despite the heavily masculine framing of war and its institutions, feminist historians have revealed the many roles women have always played in war as leaders, camp makers, fighters, carers, supporters and objectors. Women's active participation in government militaries and armed groups is also increasingly the norm today. Women politicians are overseeing defence ministries in eleven countries today and women are playing active roles in many state and non-state military forces, even if they are often bullied and sexually harassed within armed forces because they are women.[2] Twenty-first-century women join military forces that have explicitly 'pro-women' policies, like Kurdish forces and Colombian armed groups. But they also join armed groups, voluntarily and forcibly, which have social policies that are inherently patriarchal and restrict women's rights.[3]

Legal Description

International law offers a minimal definition of war even if it has much to say about its conduct. The legal definition focuses on the nature of the parties and territories involved to come up with two main kinds of conflict: international armed conflicts (IAC), which are fought between two or more states, and non-international armed conflicts (NIAC), which are fought between the state and armed rebels within its territory, or between armed groups in a single state.

NIACs are, of course, more commonly known as civil wars. Lawyers officially qualify violence within a state as a NIAC when they judge that that conflict has reached a certain level of violent 'intensity' and when the parties opposing a state have significant levels of 'political organization', like organized military units, command and control (C2) functions, and control of territory. This distinguishes war's violence from non-war rioting, violent crime and civil disturbance. NIACs can be legally complicated by becoming internationalized civil wars in which other states, and armed groups from other states, join in the fight. International and non-international armed conflict can then be happening simultaneously in the same territory, as is the case today in Syria and Yemen for example. Both IACs and NIACs can also involve a third dimension, which is the 'occupation' of all or part of one state's territory by an opposing warring party. Law acknowledges such occupation as a particular context of conflict, and one that carries particular legal responsibilities.

International lawyers use Latin to describe the reasons for war as the *ad bellum* aspects of war—the arguments used to justify going 'to war'. Wars of aggression are illegal under the UN Charter and going to war is only legal for two reasons: self-defence, or in support of a forceful military intervention mandated by the UN Security Council to maintain international peace and security. Once at war, lawyers talk about warring parties' responsibilities *in bello*, i.e. 'in war', especially their conduct of hostilities. Here they must abide by the laws of war, known more commonly today as International Humanitarian Law (IHL), which is found in the 1949 Geneva Conventions, their two Additional Protocols of 1977 and other international standards.

Political Description

The legal description of warfare is not a full political, military or social description of war. Instead, the laws of war are primarily designed to hold the authorities of warring parties legally responsible for war in the clearest way possible. War is more truly described by its political purpose (the reasons why people go to war), its military characteristics (the scale, strategy and tactics of the fight), and its socio-economic impact (its effect on people and society). Viewing war politically and militarily reveals several different kinds of war that we have seen this century and can expect in decades to come.

Back in 1941, during World War II, the sociologist Hans Speier, described three main types of war, each of which has a distinct political intent and can be easily found in today's wars. *Absolute war* is intent upon the annihilation of an enemy—the total destruction or conquest of a people or political movement, like today's conflict against the Muslim minority in Myanmar's Rakhine region and the strategy many states show towards the Islamic State group. *Instrumental war* is fought to achieve a particular strategic advantage of territory, wealth or power, like the US invasion of Iraq, and Russia's annexation of Crimea and its war in Ukraine. *Agonistic war* is fought as a regulated contest between current champions to see who should rightly take control as the sole ruler of a political space or economic resource, as we see in Yemen and in the regional struggle for dominance between Iran and Saudi Arabia.

More simply still, modern security experts distinguish between two types of war: *war of choice* and *war of survival*. A war of choice is a war that you choose to fight for some strategic advantage or to stop the military advance and political expansion of a distant enemy or the low-grade enemy of an ally. These are not essential wars in which the existence of your own state or people is truly threatened. A war of survival, by contrast, is a conflict in which a state or a group is fighting for its political existence or even its very human existence as a group. Wars of survival tend to become *total war* in which every aspect of the state or group is mobilized to win. Obviously, what may be a war of choice for one side can be a war of survival for the other, just as a Great Power's small war may be a very big and total war for its enemy. These descriptions of political intent as annihilation and survival, advantage and competition, are useful headline categories to explain the political logics behind the general reasons why states and armed groups decide on war as policy, and then use it against their enemies.

The terms *asymmetric war* and *peer-to-peer war* were coined in the 1970s. They, too, are useful general terms to describe strategic power dynamics once enemies are at war.[4] They describe the different power relations and military shape of a fight. These are recognizable from great myths, like the ancient asymmetric fight between David and Goliath, or contests of equals like Gilgamesh and Enkidu, and Karna and Arjuna. Asymmetric warfare is war in which one side is militarily much bigger and better than the other. This forces the militarily weaker side to find advantage in asymmetric strategies where their smallness gives them a big advantage. Strategies of assassination, sabotage, terrorizing attacks and propaganda assaults side-step their enemy's conventional military advantage to knock them off balance in other ways. Peer-to-peer or *near-peer* warfare is a contest between forces that are relatively equal in strength and skill. As we will see, this form of warfare is now uppermost in the planning and preparations of major powers and it looks set to dictate the development of warfare in the next ten years of the century.

War today is used to pursue a range of political purposes that are ancient, enduring and certainly not new to this century. *Supremacist identity wars,* like this century's militant Islamist revival and the resulting Global War on Terror, involve one or both sides asserting racial, tribal, religious or value-based supremacy over an enemy and being intent on expelling, eradicating, punishing, converting or subjugating them. Islamist struggle also has a strong element of *ideological revolutionary war* in which one side rises up against another to assert its own ideology and topple the existing political establishment, while also mobilizing 'the people' to change their ways and fall in line with their ideology. Revolutionary wars involve a struggle for the 'hearts and minds' of whole populations and have been a key element of wars fought by Islamists and their liberal or authoritarian opponents in Afghanistan and many countries across the Middle East and the Sahel.

*Self-determination and liberation war*s tend to be more expressly territorial but equally focused on political identity. They see a self-defined people rise up on a land to resist a governing power and achieve political recognition as an independent state or autonomous region within a state. Myanmar has several long-running wars of this type where

Kachin, Keren and Rakhine people are fighting for autonomy. Self-determination may also include a revolutionary ideology when people want a specifically liberal, socialist or Islamist nation. These wars often involve *annexation, occupation and resistance* as enemies capture, or refuse to give up, a disputed territory. This century's long wars between Palestinians and Israelis, Moroccans and Sahrawis, Indians and Pakistanis over Kashmir, or Singhalese and Tamils in Sri Lanka are conflicts of this kind. So, too, is the new war between Russia and Ukraine over the Crimea and Donbass regions, and the latent contest between China and Taiwan.

In *hegemonic contest wars*, regional or global powers fight peers, directly or through proxies, to establish their dominance over a political arena, as the USA, Russia, Iran and Saudi Arabia are doing in the Middle East, as competing Ethiopian powers are doing today in and around Tigray, and as with China and the US in the newly coined 'Indo–Pacific'. Many wars mix these different political purposes. So, for example, the war between Russia and Ukraine can also be read as a key piece of the wider hegemonic contest between Russia and NATO.

Military coups and repressive dictatorships, as in Myanmar today, are another variant of war in which military units seize power and then govern with armed force. Much warfare today is also a routine form of *predation and raiding* that lasts for decades. This is politically minimal war of violent plunder and theft in which elite leaders, state forces and armed groups wage war as much for economic gain as for political ends, usually using armed violence to steal from the state and civilian population. Even if they also have political causes, wars in Myanmar, Afghanistan, Nigeria, Iraq, Libya, the Central African Republic, South Sudan and the Democratic Republic of Congo (DRC) also have a strong commercial logic around forcefully extracting natural resources, informal taxation, forced sex and marriage. These constant raiding wars produce a chronic condition of 'no war, no peace' as armed political parties routinely clash for decades over (deliberately) failing peace processes while benefiting from politically organized crime and alternating power-sharing agreements. This chronic violence, which spikes sporadically then falls below the legal threshold of an 'armed conflict', is a pervasive form of war today and is well described as 'political unsettlement' by Professor Christine Bell.[5]

Finally, amidst many of these situations of chronic political unsettlement, UN forces are mandated to wage *UN wars of protection and state-building* in support of internationally agreed peace processes or to protect civilians in conflict. Depending on the mandate given to them by the UN Security Council, this can involve UN forces fighting directly as a party to the war, or trying to re-shape armed politics with weak military deterrent and soft power alone.

Ten Characteristics of War Today

Watching wars from afar and reading about them in ICRC headquarters and in university libraries, I see ten clear characteristics in early twenty-first-century warfare. These are not all original to war today but help to explain the form warfare has taken in the first twenty-one years of the century.

1. Militarily Small Wars

First, wars today are militarily small. There are no huge land armies sweeping through continents, nor large navies and air forces constantly clashing with one another in campaigns that kill millions of military personnel and civilians alike. Large conventional warfare is rare today. There have been very few major battles between large forces, and none that has got close to the scale of Solferino, or to industrial warfare's huge bombing and battles of the two world wars and those that followed in Korea and Vietnam. Analysing conflict data in 2009, Professor Erik Melander noted that 'battle severity and civilians killed in civil conflicts have significantly decreased since the end of the Cold War'.[6]

Although the number of wars has been increasing, this trend of militarily small wars with relatively small numbers of violent battle deaths has continued through the 2010s, with exceptions in Syria and Iraq. In Syria, combatant and civilian battle deaths have been higher than most. In Iraq, the Battle of Mosul in 2016 stands out as 'worthy of Stalingrad itself', according to urban warfare expert

17

Professor Anthony King. In seven months of fighting in Mosul, an Iraqi armed force of 94,000 with US support took on a much smaller ISg (Islamic State group) force of up to 12,000 fighters who combined various formations of street fighting with many thousands of IEDs and booby traps, individual suicide bombers, and 482 suicide vehicle attacks that packed explosives into civilian vehicles to achieve large wide-area explosions. Most of the city was destroyed. Most of the ISg fighters were killed. A conservative estimate gives 1,400 Iraqi soldiers killed and 7,000 wounded. Between 3,500 and 25,000 civilians are estimated to have been killed, with no real precision on these numbers as yet.[7]

Most battles this century have been much smaller than Mosul. The century opened with the US invasion of Afghanistan in 2001, which did involve major air attacks on Kabul, Kandahar and Jalalabad but soon reverted to an asymmetric form of insurgency and counter-insurgency. The Afghan War has been fought out at battalion and company level, with precision air support on the US side, and not by great corps and divisions. The Taliban has combined company- and platoon-level confrontations with roadside explosive devices and attacks against civilians.

The invasion of Iraq in 2003 stands out as a clash of two large armies, but not for very long because US military superiority rapidly overwhelmed Iraqi forces. There have been urban battles in other Iraqi cities, like Baghdad, Fallujah and Ramadi, and in Syria in Aleppo and Homs, which have seen medium-sized conventional forces deployed against smaller and comparatively poorly equipped opponents. For example, the second battle of Fallujah in 2004 took place in a city of 250,000 people, most of whom had fled. It involved 18,000 US-led ground forces using artillery, tanks and infantry, with fire support from air and sea, against a force estimated at 4,500 Iraqi and foreign fighters.[8] US-led forces lost 110 people killed and several hundred wounded. The opposing armed groups lost heavily with 3,000 people killed or captured.[9]

Yemen has seen similar urban battles. ACLED (Armed Conflict Location and Event Data Project) estimates that between January 2015 and June 2019, a total of 90,000 people were killed violently in Yemen's war. The majority of these were combatants with an estimated 12,000 civilians violently killed. The most deadly areas were the long urban battles in Taiz and Hodeidah. Taiz developed as a long fight between several armed groups, with an estimated 18,419 violent deaths over four-and-a-half years, including 2,282 civilians. The battle for Hodeidah, which escalated in 2018 with a surge of 2,000 troops from the United Arab Emirates, had total fatalities estimated at 10,000 during the same period. The first year of the war was the most lethal for civilians because of consistently indiscriminate air strikes by the Saudi air force. ACLED's estimate of 4,468 civilian deaths in 2015 is twice its estimate for 2018, which is the next most violent year, and shows a change of tactics by the Saudi air force.

Nevertheless, ACLED estimates that 67% of Yemeni violent civilian deaths were the result of Saudi air strikes.[10]

Yemen's 12,000 civilian violent deaths over four-and-a-half years compares, for example, to 45,000 civilians killed in a single night in Hamburg by Allied bombing in 1943, an estimated 560,000 Chinese civilians killed by Japanese bombing during their invasion and occupation of China in the 1930s, and probably 3 million civilians violently killed in strategic bombings, massacres and executions in the Korean War in the 1950s.[11] The difference in the scale of military violence between our century and the twentieth century is thankfully and dramatically different, so far.

Syria is the world's worst war this century on many counts and has seen ten years of conventional fighting. This has often been led from the air in brutal twentieth-century style using unguided bombs and widely fragmenting barrel bombs and cluster bombs, which have killed thousands of civilians and enemy fighters and destroyed whole areas of Syrian cities like Homs, Damascus and Aleppo. Yet, in military terms, the forces have still been relatively small, and ultimately one-sided since the Russians entered the fight in 2015. Facing no competing air power, the Russians have also stood back from the fight and deployed a light military footprint. They have had an average of 4,000 people on the ground at any one time, most of whom were logistical and technical support. The Russians achieved their military objectives through air power, and by better command and control (C2) of Syrian and Iranian forces, which were supported by Iraqi militia and about 2,000 well-trained mercenaries from Wagner Group, the leading Russian private military company (PMC). Like Western forces, they also used special forces in advanced target identification, punitive raids and forceful initial attacks to 'soften up' and confuse the enemy frontline before larger ground offences. The Russian air force contingent was small. It averaged about 35 planes (bombers, heavy fighters and transport) and 17 helicopters, occasionally supported by large cruise missiles fired from the Caspian and Black seas. Russian involvement has proved decisive, with only 90 Russian casualties and the loss of 8 planes (only 1 in combat) and 8 helicopters.[12] Russia has won using a small and low-cost military force that supports the ground forces of its allies in a war that has been disastrous for millions.

Most twenty-first-century wars in the US-led Global War on Terror have been a similar asymmetric struggle between high-tech Western forces and their allies against largely low-tech ground forces. War has largely been pursued as insurgency and counter-insurgency, with insurgents tending to avoid force-on-force clashes and preferring indirect methods of attack—like ambushes, roadside mines, IEDs, snipers, sabotage, kidnapping and the deliberate mass killing and displacement of civilian populations across a wide area. This humiliates the opposition and requires enemy forces to cover wide areas. Guerrilla forces always prefer to have their enemies spread thinly so they are over-stretched and easier to take on at platoon or company level, as the Taliban so often did in Afghanistan.

NATO, UN and US-led forces in Afghanistan, Somalia, Iraq and Libya, and their specially installed government partners, have spent two decades trying to implement effective regime change and liberal state-building through 'stabilization' and 'pacification' operations, which try to win over the civilian population and improve their lives with liberal social policies and state-building investment. French-led forces are now leading similar counter-insurgencies against Jihadist forces across the Sahel in Mali, Niger and Burkina Faso. These Western-led counter-insurgencies draw on imperial playbooks from nineteenth- and twentieth-century colonization wars, in which Britain and France invaded Africa or formed post-Ottoman states in West Asia, or on US counter-insurgency manuals for the Vietnam War and other decolonization wars in the 1950s and 1960s.

Much military activity in African wars today involves the strategic raiding, terrorizing and displacing of civilian communities by small-scale infantry units.[13] In South Sudan, the DRC, the CAR and Nigeria, warfare has continued as a traditional form of political contest and raiding war that involves the destruction of villages, the takeover of water and grazing areas, the killing of men, the rape of women and the abduction of girls and cattle. Around towns, raiding involves more urban pillage of vehicles and electronic equipment. Area control across countryside and cities is maintained by patrol, checkpoints, forcible taxing, intimidation and repeated raids to suppress resistance. These tactics are often deployed by government forces and armed groups alike.

All these wars are militarily small for three main reasons. First, because most of the military protagonists are small, and the Great Powers involved—the USA, Russia and NATO forces—are not fighting each other directly, even when they are on opposing sides. These major powers have only confronted small forces and so rarely need to fight at scale but operate a counter-insurgency strategy instead. China, the world's third largest military power, has not gone to war this century.

The second reason is that the major powers prefer to keep war small and computerized precision technology enables them to do so. Scarred by the invasions and occupations at the beginning of the century, and haunted by Vietnam and Afghanistan last century, US, NATO and Russian forces want to avoid a large footprint. They prefer a 'light footprint' and more 'remote warfare' that combines stand-off missiles, drones, special forces, proxy forces and a training-and-support role to their allies—the military equivalent of 'localization' in humanitarian aid. This is preferred because, currently, the Great Powers want to avoid a direct clash and they put a high value on 'force protection' and do not want large losses of their military personnel.

The third reason these wars are militarily small is that the USA and NATO have adopted a military policy and rules of engagement (RoE) that respect the laws of war and deliberately seek to minimize civilian harm and destruction. They want to fight as humanely and honourably as possible. For the moment, at least, this is their military culture and what their electorates expect.

2. Religious Wars with a Muslim Geography

Geography and religious intent are the next clear trend in current wars. War this century has mainly spread across West Asia and West Africa, with persistent outbreaks also in South Asia, Europe and Central Asia. Within this geography is a demographic trend that war has been fought mostly in Muslim majority countries since 2003. Some 65% of war is taking place in states with majority Muslim populations, and a majority of armed groups are made up of Muslim fighters or have emphatically Jihadist revolutionary ideologies. This has led American professor Barbara Walter to describe today's civil wars as a 'third wave' in the modern history of civil war. Today's Islamist revolutionary wave follows two earlier nineteenth- and twentieth-century waves of nationalist identity war and communist class-based revolutionary war.[14]

Like communist revolutionary warfare before it, today's Islamist wave has transnational ambitions that hopes for regional and global revolution, and not just the transformation of one or two states. This means that two global forces—Jihadist revolutionaries and their state enemies—are fighting the same meta-war for and against Islamist revolution in many different countries round the world. The USA, UK and France are the Western states most active in confronting Jihadism, either working separately or through NATO and the UN.

3. Internationalized Civil Wars of Armed Groups and Coalitions

A third striking trend is that most war since 2010 takes the form of internationalized civil wars with a large number of state and non-state opponents in coalitions on each side. Early twenty-first-century war is increasingly crowded, and many different states, armed groups and PMCs join in on one side or another. As we have seen, powerful states prefer to keep their military footprint light and focus on remote warfare in which they use remote weapons and enable local proxy forces instead of taking centre stage on the battlefield themselves.

Dunant would have understood coalitions of states, but he would be extremely surprised by the large numbers of armed groups in twenty-first-century wars. More non-state armed groups have emerged in the last eight years than in the previous eight decades, and there are hundreds, probably thousands, of different armed groups fighting on today's battlefields and in the information space around them.

Dunant's own ICRC currently has contacts with 465 armed groups around the world in its humanitarian efforts to reach people in need.[15] Professor Brian McQuinn, an expert on armed groups, has studied their different types of organizational dynamics. Some groups, like FARC (Revolutionary Armed Forces of Colombia), ISg and the New People's Army, are large and highly organized, with a vertical command structure that sees power and orders flowing down from a designated leadership. A distinctive feature of the large Islamist groups, like ISg and Al Qaeda, is that they have transnational ambitions and so fight around the world, from the Far East, through West Asia, across the Sahel, and in the West in Paris, London and, of course, New York. They are global armed groups like their anarchist, communist and Maoist predecessors in the twentieth century, who also worked in global networks with international ambitions. However, the great majority of today's armed groups are not so organized and ambitious. Instead, they function more horizontally with 'diffuse leadership and authority… acting more like disruptive start-ups than standard corporations', and often falling into factions, changing alliances or dissolving over the course of long conflicts.[16] Many originate as 'micro-groups' of twenty people and then build coalitions with other groups to scale-up their forces and coordinate attacks while profiting from a decentralized structure that protects their cause from being 'decapitated' by the killing of a major leader. As ever, most armed groups fighting an asymmetric war of resistance against larger high-tech forces are wise to develop 'network strength', which is more resilient to pressure than a transparent hierarchical organization.

Coalition warfare in places like Syria, Iraq, Yemen, Libya and Mali makes battle spaces extremely congested, with several different governments bombing from the air, launching special forces operations on the ground, and training, advising and supplying dozens of allies and proxies. This crowding can increase exponentially as armed groups splinter and take a separate identity to fight their primary enemy, while often bearing a secondary grudge against their former comrades. On the ground, this can create a labyrinth of different sectors, checkpoints, flags and insignia. More importantly, the complexity and mutation of coalitions can lead to a dangerous dilution of military responsibility and inconsistency in military conduct across coalition battle spaces. Some warring parties may feel no obligation to live up to the laws of war respected by their coalition allies if they are miles away and a long way down the chain of command. Law-abiding coalition partners may also struggle with an out-of-sight out-of-mind mentality towards government forces and armed groups they train in advance, or supply and support from the air, but are never close to at the frontline.[17]

A mosaic of territorial control by armed groups means that many millions of people in conflict countries live their lives in areas 'beyond the State' in war today. Here, government services struggle to reach them or deliberately cut them off as enemies. Separate 'rebel governance' then develops, often as a deliberate goal of war, as in the 'Caliphate' set up by ISg in Syria and Iraq, and large areas controlled by FARC in Colombia.

4. Urban Warfare

Territorial governance gives armed groups areas to defend and an incentive to govern them sufficiently well to avoid the need to open a second front to counter resistance to their rule. This changes their tactics because to defend their territory they must be able and willing to fight conventional battles to defend urban areas.[18] Urban warfare has, therefore, become another deep trend in the last twenty years in contrast to the largely rural insurgencies that characterized twentieth-century civil wars. Urban warfare combines ferocious air and artillery bombardment, tanks, street fighting, snipers, booby traps and badly damaged essential infrastructure. The century so far has seen significant conventional military confrontations in cities and towns like Gaza, Fallujah, Benghazi, Raqqa, Aleppo and Mosul, between state and non-state forces, and frequently between rival armed groups in towns in Libya, northern Mali and Yemen.

Urban warfare poses terrible difficulties for civilian populations and puts them at especial risk from physical injury and from impoverishment and disease because of the destruction of electricity networks, water supply systems, markets, shops and banks, health services and schools. It also poses real difficulties for armed forces who want to respect the laws of war but need to win an urban battle. The density of population in towns and cities makes difficult the separation of civilian areas and military installations; and key supply lines, energy and water infrastructure are often 'dual-use'—serving military and civilian needs—and so prone to attack. The most devastating damage in urban warfare comes from the use of wide-impact explosive weapons in densely populated areas. Explosives fired from artillery, handheld rocket launchers, drones, planes or ships cause severe blast and fragmentation. Even precision strikes have imprecise blast. And many artillery and air strikes in war are not made with precision weapons but with unguided barrel bombs and older generation artillery that often have no reasonable prospect, or intention, of discriminate targeting.

The sheer force of blast alone can kill and injure people over a radius of many metres by blowing them off their feet, fracturing their bones and cutting their bodies on surrounding buildings with resulting horrendous open wounds. Blast can also blow people's internal organs apart in deadly internal injuries or 'closed wounds'. When this blast is also filled with fragments from the bomb itself and from concrete, metal and glass from the buildings and vehicles it has destroyed, then it becomes more deadly still, with chunks and fragments cutting right through people. Blast fragments also destroy water pipes, electricity lines, homes and shops. One small blast fragment can smash a water pipe or an electricity substation and stop supply to thousands of people for weeks. This causes considerable suffering to thousands of people in a neighbourhood by cutting water and electricity supply to homes, hospitals and schools miles from the target.

In 2019, the *Explosive Violence Monitor* recorded 17,904 civilian casualties from explosive weapons used in populated areas in all wars around the world.[19] This is a lot of men, women and children horribly killed and hurt in one year. Thankfully, it is a small number compared, for example, to the 40,000 civilians killed in the UK alone in the seven-month Blitz in 1940–1, or the hundreds of thousands of civilians blown up in US Cold War bombing in Korea and Vietnam. Today's figures show clear signs of a new ethical commitment by Western forces this century to avoid bombing civilians, and a relative lack of air power in most wars today.

The experience of Filipino armed forces at the Battle of Marawi from June to December 2017 shows how explosive weapons and urban damage are still militarily necessary even after the evacuation of most of the civilian population.[20] Thankfully, this six-month battle began with the organized evacuation of 250,000 civilians coordinated by religious leaders and the government. This was followed by the advance of a significant Filipino force of three brigades, which moved carefully into the city to dislodge and defeat highly organized and militarily effective Jihadist armed groups. But the battle was hard and costly for government forces, and widely destructive of part of the city. The Jihadists had clear situational advantage via a system of underground cellars and tunnels below the city and had clear 'overwatch' from high buildings whenever government forces moved along the ground, up streets and along alleys. This overwatch gave the Jihadists real-time intelligence of troop movements, which they also enhanced by using hobby drones, and the advantage of deadly sniper fire. They had no reservations about using rocket-propelled grenades (RPGs) and laced every street and building with IEDs to kill as many government soldiers as possible.

Responsible armed forces must do everything they can to reduce warfare's indiscriminate effect in urban areas, but destructive urban warfare will still happen wherever a rival force is deeply dug into strategic urban space and determined to hold it at all costs. In Marawi, this meant that government forces had to proceed slowly, building by building, to dislodge and kill their enemies. Taking each building required explosive weapons to be fired into every room, either by artillery or precision air power, to kill Jihadists within it and to trigger the many IEDs that would otherwise kill Filipino forces when they fought their way inside. In the damaged streets, Filipino military engineers also had to use explosives to blow pathways between rubble and damaged buildings to enable the advance. The battle was costly in military lives and injuries, with 978 Jihadists killed and 168 Filipino military killed and 1,400 injured. The Filipino government advance was reliant on high explosives for its force protection, and other armed forces will have little choice but to pursue explosives-based tactics in urban warfare in the years to come. Precision weapons can reduce urban destruction but not eradicate it. If civilian populations are unable to flee in advance, then urban warfare will continue to be lethal for people, as it has been in Middle East wars.

5. Long War

Long war is a clear characteristic of most wars today, which are frequently called 'protracted conflicts' or 'forever wars'. But war has always been long as well as short. The first war to be chronicled in great detail by a historian, Thucydides, was the Peloponnesian War between Athens and Sparta which lasted for 27 years in the fifth century BCE. England and France had a war that lasted for 116 years between 1337 and 1453, known as the Hundred Years War. China has known very long periods of war. Last century, its people endured 38 years of civil war after the Empire collapsed in 1911 and before the Communist Party took power in 1949. This came after the long 'century of humiliation' when China faced constant confrontation with imperial European powers, and the Taiping and Boxer Rebellions. Short wars happen, too. Both world wars were relatively short. Israel and its Arab rivals famously had a Six-Day War in 1967, and in 2020 Armenia and Azerbaijan had a war that lasted for 45 days. But most wars are long and last for years and decades rather than days, weeks or months. One of the persistent illusions about war is an over-confidence that 'it will be over by Christmas'. It very rarely is, and there are probably four main reasons why wars are long today, as they often have been in earlier centuries.

The first reason is because, in reality, wars are violent spikes in deeper political conflicts. Many historians will tell you that England's deep conflict with France actually started with the Norman Conquest in 1066 and only really ended in 1904 when they made peace in an Entente Cordiale in the face of an increasingly powerful Germany. Similarly, the Six-Day War was one violent spike in an entrenched conflict between Arabs and Jews that started in the 1920s and continues violently today as another hundred years war.

The second reason that wars are long today is because the reasons for them often mutate as the war goes along. A war that starts about oil or humanitarian protection becomes a war of jihad and self-determination. New warring parties arise with new interests and new grievances. New allies join in to widen the conflict and new events arise, like recession or political changes back home, which weaken a previously dominant ally. New leaders appear with the political and military genius to reframe the struggle and reverse the flow of war.

War in Afghanistan, for example, has mutated repeatedly. Afghanistan has been in almost constant war since 1979—some 42 years. War started with a Russian invasion and a resistance struggle against it. With Russian withdrawal in 1989, the war then morphed into a civil war between the Islamist Taliban, which had been part of the resistance struggle against the Russians, and its tribal rivals against more secular-minded opponents, until the Taliban eventually took power in 1996. The US invasion in 2001 and its deposing of the Taliban started a new period of war and resistance that lasted until the Taliban's victory in 2021. Similarly long mutating wars exist in countries like Iraq, Yemen, Syria, Nigeria and the Democratic Republic of Congo. In contrast, some long conflicts can remain resolutely mono-causal. Like the Israeli–Palestinian conflict or the Sri Lankan Civil War, they follow the same single cause for decades.

Longevity becomes intentional when wars mutate into a mutually beneficial stalemate that suits all sides because they can use its violence to generate great profits or are equally determined to resist political settlements imposed by outsiders. Professor David Keen has described the phenomenon of 'useful enemies' in wars in South Sudan and Sierra Leone and in the many counter-terrorism wars of Western states and has shown how warring parties often cooperate to keep wars going if instability, weak government and a permanent state of emergency serve their purposes.[21] In northern Nigeria today, government forces and rebels are both ruthless to civilians and find profit in the conflict.

Thirdly, history tells us that asymmetric wars are long because they are often unwinnable. Decolonization wars at the end of European empires between the 1950s and the 1970s were asymmetrical conflicts like today's. They were fought out for many years between zealous insurgents and more high-tech colonial powers in places like Indonesia, Vietnam and Laos, Algeria, Kenya, Namibia and Zimbabwe. These wars were essentially unwinnable by either side because they were militarily unwinnable for the insurgents and politically unsustainable for the colonialists, whose citizens and allies wanted them to stop. They were, therefore, not militarily resolved and only ended by face-saving withdrawals by imperial powers who implemented hasty independence arrangements on the way out. We have seen similarly asymmetric time horizons in Afghanistan. Here, the Taliban had an indefinite time horizon for victory and so could deploy deep strategic patience and confidence in an eventual triumph in a long war. In contrast, the USA and NATO simply ran out of time and political patience, and they abandoned the fight. Strategic patience combined with deft military and political leadership can, therefore, win asymmetric wars, as the Taliban has shown. So, too, can extreme asymmetric force. Counter-insurgents pursuing absolute war and an annihilation policy have beaten otherwise resilient insurgents, as the Sri Lankan government did in their ruthless 2009 victory over the Tamil Tigers.

Lastly, wars are long when they embody 'radical disagreements' with diametrically opposing truths that make them genuinely insoluble by negotiation and mutual accommodation.[22] Islamist or 'Jihadist' conflicts, which make up the majority of twenty-first-century conflicts, are deeply resistant to negotiation and compromise because extreme Islamist revolutionary convictions permit no halfway positions on core religious commitments or supremacist theocratic politics. Liberal and authoritarian enemies of Jihadists are equally resistant to core compromises with Islamism: hence the impossibility of negotiation. Monica Toft's tracking of data on religious civil war shows it to have higher levels of 'deadliness' and longevity than non-religious war in recent decades.[23] Deep conflicts over territory, like the Israeli–Palestinian conflict and the Moroccan–Polisario conflict, are also close to zero-sum disputes of territory and ideology. And, of course, the Israeli–Palestinian conflict has a strong religious dimension, too, in the mindsets of Zionist settlers and Palestinian Islamists.

6. Chronic Political Violence

The most pervasive form of violence experienced by people around the world is an agonizing limbo between war and peace. Millions of people live in an undefined political state described by Roger Mac Ginty as 'no war, no peace', where the gun and political repression are a key part of everyday politics. This volatile condition is daily life in places like Lebanon, Somalia, South Sudan, CAR, Libya and Iraq, where imposed peace processes continuously fail and armed politicians and their followers alternate between political negotiations and violent flare-ups to secure a better place in government and business. Here, people live in war-like conditions 'mired in insecurity, chronic poverty and the persistence of factors that sparked and sustained civil war'.[24] Dictatorship is often similar. In Myanmar and Belarus, dictatorships routinely use military violence, detention and torture to suppress dissent.

Some wars today are not called wars at all because states prefer to pretend they merely have policing problems. In El Salvador, Mexico, Brazil and South Africa millions of people live in war-like conditions with astonishingly high numbers of violent deaths. International lawyers are reluctant to categorize these situations as armed conflicts because such judgements will be robustly contested by powerful governments. But they could easily meet the legal description. Drug cartels and gangs, which drive so much of this violence, are politically motivated to kill or co-opt political power and dominate territory. Their armed groups are sufficiently organized to meet the threshold of an armed force and are routinely countered by the military rather than police. Yet, states prefer that this is 'criminality' and 'urban violence', even when the annual death rates from shootings in Mexico and Brazil for 2013 were higher than the first two years of the death toll of the Syrian war. In contrast, the traditional gang violence of cattle-raiding in South Sudan is often called war; so, too, is Boko Haram's armed raiding and abduction of young women in northeast Nigeria, which continues a long tradition of criminal political violence in that border area. If such violence were in Brazil or Russia, it might be called armed violence, organized crime and human trafficking, but not war.

Professor Keith Krause has studied violent deaths across the world and draws four surprising conclusions:

> most lethal violence does not occur in war zones; the majority of states most affected by lethal violence are not at war; the level of violence in some non-conflict settings is higher than in war zones, and much of this violence is organized and in some sense political.[25]

Venezuela, Honduras and El Salvador are more dangerous places to live in than Afghanistan, and their people suffer levels of displacement that characterize war zones. Some officially recognized wars are certainly not the worst places to live. Many Hondurans might find the quiet parts of Damascus a great improvement on San Pedro Sula. The legal definition of war is applied selectively and politically. Sometimes it is narrowly applied when states would rather not be described as 'conflict-affected' and have their politics discussed by the UN Security Council. Sometimes the war label is generously applied, especially when Western militaries and humanitarian agencies, in particular, would like to get involved.

Because of the political vagaries of defining war, the UN is now using the Heidelberg Institute's wider frame of 'political conflict' to capture the extent of organized political violence around the world today. This uses five categories of conflict, three of which are expressly violent to different degrees of intensity: violent crisis; limited war; and war. Heidelberg's more general monitoring of political conflict is indeed a better way to understand the prevalence of armed violence in many people's lives across the globe, including the gun violence in the USA and 'frozen' conflicts across Europe, like in Cyprus and Northern Ireland.[26] Looking ahead, as Clionadh Raleigh has argued, it seems clear that political violence is rising faster and spreading more pervasively across the world than formal war, and may well be a bigger challenge to political order and human wellbeing.[27] The state-centric legal idea of war is looking a little old fashioned: it does not capture most of the organized violence that is killing and impoverishing people today.

7. Computerized Warfare

The changing technological character of war is the most original feature of twenty-first-century war because it brings real novelty to warfare. Military technology has developed in every generation, but computerized technology and artificial intelligence (AI) put the world at the beginning of a new technological trajectory. Paul Scharre has done a great job in showing how today's wars already involve highly computerized new-tech warfare, especially in the sophisticated armed forces of major powers. His analysis shows we are now close to very high levels of autonomy in which war machines are not simply programmed to pre-set rules and targets but are significantly autonomous as 'goal-based and self-directed' weapons systems without a human 'in the loop' of their immediate operations.[28]

Most military fighting platforms, like planes, tanks and ships, are no longer the complicated mechanical machines of industrial warfare. They are highly complex 'systems of systems' automated with extraordinary precision and speed well beyond the understanding of the human operator and intricately merged with other units in the wider fighting system. An average 1930s fighter aircraft was made up of hundreds of different components. In the 1950s this rose to tens of thousands of components, and in the last decade this has risen to 300,000 components in the F-35 fighter aircraft plus 5.6 million lines of computer code to make it work.[29] Because of the prevalence of asymmetric warfare, these high-tech weapons operate in the same battle spaces as bolt-action Lee Enfield rifles in Afghanistan, initially designed by the British in 1897 and using ammunition saved from World War II, and the Kalashnikov automatic weapons designed and made in the Cold War that are common across Africa and all other wars.[30]

Like any modern company or public service, the back-office functions of a modern military force are fully digitalized and use artificial intelligence of various kinds in their HR, logistics, finance and security systems. On the frontline, AI-enabled surveillance and weapons are well on their way to achieving critical mass in warfare. Most obvious and ubiquitous is the drone, which is an unmanned [sic] vehicle that moves through land, sea or air. Drones may be armed or unarmed and are used for surveillance, attack and defence. Often, they work as part of 'loitering' systems and stay in the same area observing, searching, reporting and firing. They can vary in size from an insect to a major airborne missile-bearing platform or small submarine, and they can operate alone or 'swarm' in packs. Drones are either remotely operated or pre-programmed and automated throughout their task, or they are a mixture of the two. Significantly, they can also vary in price and sophistication so that they are being used by armed groups as well as state forces, and off-the-shelf commercial drones can be adapted for military purposes. Drone warfare is now a routine and effective instrument of war. For example, Turkish drones were decisive in Azerbaijan's quick and comprehensive victory over Armenia in 2020.

But drones are just the most visible aspect of new-tech warfare today. They are also the most controversial, perhaps, for being used as the weapon of choice in targeted killings in the US fight against Jihadist groups, in recent Iranian attacks on the Saudi oilfields, in permanently hovering Israeli surveillance over Gaza, and in the US killing of an Iranian general in Baghdad. More invisible, and mainstreamed into all modern military forces, is the routine digitalization of AI-based systems of surveillance, analysis, attack and defence. AI is fundamentally an enabler of decision-making in new weapons systems to date. It is not a weapon in itself. But it is already changing war by making it exponentially faster, especially in systems of automated sensing, intelligence-gathering and targeting. AI systems can rapidly gather and process intelligence and locational data to offer real-time scenario building on troop movements, civilian presence, route-planning and attack impact, and then function as 'recommender systems' that advise operational commanders on real-time scenarios and tactical options on the battlefield.[31]

War has traditionally involved human and non-human combinations—for example, human–animal interaction in cavalry and human–machine interaction in tanks and planes—but today the continuous fibre of all high-end military operations is human–computer interaction (HCI).[32] This century's combatants are physically fused with computers and are 'riding laptop' into war after centuries of riding horseback. Combatants now routinely use a computer tablet linked to a satellite to call in and target air strikes in support of infantry operations, or they use the text message of a mobile phone to set off an IED. They communicate instantly with comrades across different battle spaces, and commanders can watch operations livestreamed in capitals thousands of miles away. Remote drone operators work from different countries and go home to their families after a busy day of bombing or surveillance. Humans and drones operating seamlessly together in 'hybrid formations' is increasingly the norm. Planes flown by human pilots fly as part of the same formation, with drones as their wingmen. Infantry and naval units work together, with drones going in advance to detect the enemy ahead and report or fire, while human troops are supplied from the rear with food and ammunition by logistics drones. Clearance of mines and unexploded ordinance is led by AI-based machines. All the time, these mixed human and robotic units are served from outer space by AI-enabled satellites ensuring their functionality and their communications with each other and with higher levels of command.

Cyber warfare is another new field of computerized warfare. Cyber is different from so-called 'kinetic' AI-based weapons, which watch people and things, or blow them up, in physical space. Cyber warfare uses digital computer systems to spy on and attack opponents in digital space in an attempt to undermine the increasingly important computerized systems that control and operate all human society. Cyber warfare is in its infancy but already in play. It operates via the internet, which is a new global commons and a classic 'dual-use' space that simultaneously manages civilian and military infrastructure, rocket systems, electricity supply, hospitals and schools. Like the physical roads of World War II, which carried the tanks of invading armies and the tractors of local farmers, the superhighway of the internet is a space of military and civilian activity. The so-called Internet of Things (IoT), which sees an increasing number of people's smart phones linked up to entry phones, TVs, water and heating systems and cars, is also dramatically increasing the potential 'surface' of a conflict. This means civilians can be attacked in their homes and through their many appliances that are connected to the global commons of the internet.[33]

Most cyber attacks today, and there are millions every day, are still considered criminal problems, but they are also directly deployed in war. The ICRC describes three types of cyber warfare today. *Exploitative operations* access other people's systems to loiter, spy on and undermine the enemy by using and misusing information it finds. *Offensive operations* disrupt, degrade and destroy the enemy's systems. *Defensive operations* work constantly to secure, patch, or upgrade their digital systems to try and make them impenetrable.[34]

Nadiya Kostyuk and Yuri Zhukov analysed this 'invisible digital front' in the wars in Ukraine and Syria. Between 2014 and 2016 in Ukraine, their study saw 1,841 cyber attacks compared to 26,289 kinetic weapons attacks. In Syria, it counted 682 cyber attacks compared with 9,282 kinetic attacks between 2011 and 2016. These attacks seemed to have two main purposes: propaganda to influence or undermine support for the enemy; and disruption by trying to sabotage enemy infrastructure and services. The study concluded that cyber warfare was rife in both wars but seemed to operate in its own competitive 'bubble'. It was not yet coordinated to deliver strategic or tactical game-changing force—a bit like air power in World War I. We can expect this to change dramatically in the next ten years as warring parties increasingly lead with cyber warfare in armed conflicts or combine it strategically and seamlessly with kinetic force.

8. Sub-threshold and Hybrid War

Sub-threshold and hybrid warfare are an important strategy in early twenty-first-century warfare. These describe a mix of measures short of all-out war, like special forces operations, espionage, assassinations, cyber attacks, disinformation campaigns, military support to proxies and election-tampering, which are deniable and often operate in a 'grey zone' below mainstream public awareness and just short of obvious acts of war. The purpose of sub-threshold and hybrid warfare is to subvert, rather than militarily overwhelm, an enemy by using information and disinformation to discredit their cause in the public consciousness, split their allies, provoke a response against their interests, confuse military formations, assassinate key leadership and sabotage infrastructure.[35]

Just as armed groups often prefer to avoid a direct confrontation, so, too, do many states. Great Powers and regional powers may have clear war aims in a political situation—to support an ally or destroy an armed group—but prefer to do this without risking a full-on military confrontation with a peer or getting bogged down as a formal insurgent, counter-insurgent or occupier. This reluctance for all-out war between major powers continues a pattern of 'war aversion' in peer rivalry situations in which war is judged too costly and so loses its value and efficiency as a continuation of politics by other means.[36] These more blurred and discreet forms of warfare are able to defend and win power and influence in limited geographies without tipping a state into full-scale war. For example, they have seen Russia reclaim Crimea and China take full control of Hong Kong without a major military confrontation. Western support to democracies against authoritarianism in countries like Ukraine and South Korea also deploys sub-threshold methods.

9. Hyperlegal Warfare

A major characteristic of early twenty-first-century war is its very legal framing and the dramatic ascendancy of 'war lawyers'.[37] War needs humanitarian restraint and has traditionally had rules of some sort. The modern era, however, is striking for a remarkable 'juridification' of war in which battle spaces are 'saturated' by international law[38] and war is politically framed as a respectable legal institution, not a ferociously violent strategy.

The development of the laws of war in the 160 years since Dunant's first Geneva Convention has seen states agreeing—in conference rooms at least—clear limits to the ways in which war is fought. International Humanitarian Law (IHL) insists that the use of military force should be proportionate and not excessive, and that indiscriminate attacks and the deliberate killing, harming, starving and forced displacement of civilians is forbidden. The law outlaws rape and sexual violence, as well as torture and inhumane treatment in war, and protects particular groups of people as distinct categories of 'protected persons'. These include civilians, displaced people and refugees, women, children, the wounded and sick, prisoners, religious personnel, journalists, impartial medics and humanitarian workers. Importantly, the law also protects the natural environment from excessive damage and ensures the provision of humanitarian relief. At the same time, however, laws around the 'conduct of hostilities' (CoH) also give warring parties the clear right to fight fiercely to win a war, and recognize the 'military necessity' of violence that can be extremely destructive of life, property and society.

Western warfare in the twenty-first century has championed IHL and so, too, have many resolutions of the

UN Security Council. This is one major reason why Western wars and UN wars have been smaller and less deadly in the last twenty years, which marks significant progress. The laws of war are protecting people every day. Early twenty-first-century warfare clearly shows that respecting the laws of war saves many lives, protects property and essential infrastructure, and improves the conditions of surviving civilians and detainees. It also protects military personnel from unnecessary slaughter. Today's Western forces self-identify as ethical and law-abiding. The law itself resonates deeply with values of restraint and compassion that are widely held across the world. But Western restraint is not simply a matter of values. Respecting IHL also has strategic logic for them in their counter-insurgency warfare and liberal state-building as they aim to win over and re-orientate a society rather than crush it. Western enthusiasm for the laws of war in the last thirty years has accelerated the juridification of war, but this enthusiasm has not been shared by more authoritarian governments and many armed groups, who have often deliberately killed and uprooted civilians.

But has Western enthusiasm for the laws of war created a mismatch between expectation and reality? Anyone entering the dense legal jungle around warfare today soon detects three serious problems with war's intense juridification: legal excess; a lack of enforcement; and constant manipulation.

The first problem is the density of laws, rules and legal culture. Professor David Kennedy rightly describes most wars in the first decade of the twenty-first century as reaching a state of 'hyperlegalism'.[39] Hundreds of pages of carefully hedged legal language in treaty articles and thousands more in legal commentary are routinely interpreted into legal guidance and rules of engagement for military commanders and their political masters. Hundreds of military lawyers and humanitarian lawyers advise military forces in peace and in war about the lawful conduct of hostilities. With its 10,000 lawyers, the US military is jokingly referred to as the biggest law firm in the world. In wealthy and sophisticated armed forces, which can afford them, military lawyers work with frontline units and as staff officers at command level to advise on the legality of targeting, strategy, tactics and humanitarian obligations towards the civilian population, prisoners and wounded. From the UN Security Council downwards, war is now publicly and diplomatically discussed by states, military forces, human rights organizations, humanitarian agencies and public commentators in a thick legal dialect.

IHL's proliferating rules and hyperlegal culture mean that details of the laws of war and their interpretation in particular contexts can be arcane and often only properly understood by the elite class of professional war lawyers. Like all bodies of law, what starts out as simple becomes increasingly complex and esoteric in actual disputes. The laws themselves are long, inscrutable, inaccessible texts, not easily used or understood either by combatants or by the people who are being bombed and attacked, and so by those who need them most. The Geneva Conventions and their Additional Protocols are especially dense: 280 pages of closely written legal language that specifies the detailed duties of warring parties much more than it affirms the rights of those who suffer war. The hedged discourse of much of the Geneva Conventions stands in stark contrast to the simple declaratory style of human rights treaties, and yet they cover many of the same basic rights to humane treatment, family, association, food, water, shelter, healthcare, education and livelihood. International Human Rights Law (IHRL) overlaps and applies simultaneously with the laws of war in conflict situations, but it is significantly underused in the shadow of the bulky *lex specialis*, or special law, of war.

The ICRC and the wider Red Cross and Red Crescent Movement have made impressive efforts over decades to communicate IHL simply to combatants and non-combatants alike, as well as to the global public. Boiling down their basic message into the indisputable maxim that 'Even war has limits', they have invested significant resources into simple visual and verbal messages, practical training and cross-cultural communications that find clear resonance between principles of humanity and protection in IHL and other systems of ethics, law and religious faith. But IHL has never been instinctively and easily taken up as a meaningful part of people's lives in war—it is seldom championed in the streets by social movements. The exception is around weapons and disarmament, where, often with inspiration and support from the Red Cross and Red Crescent Movement, people's movements have arisen to call for a ban on certain weapons, like landmines and nuclear weapons, or set limits to the arms trade in the Arms Trade Treaty (ATT). Significant success has also been had in creating stronger law against sexual violence as a particular crime in war. But the more complicated legal area around the conduct of hostilities, which regulates when, where and how it is legal to kill people in war, and to destroy their surroundings, remains opaque to the majority of people enduring war.

The second flaw in war's hyperlegal character today is the weakness of enforcement. The law of war is an area of international law where there is no irresistible judicial or political incentive to comply, either as a government or an armed group. In theory, there is a comprehensive system of enforcement that combines domestic law, in which international treaties like the Geneva Conventions are typically embedded, with the International Criminal Court (ICC), which operates as a court of last resort to bring individuals to account when states fail to do so. In reality, politics dictates this system. Many warring states and armed groups will not bring their own force's actions to domestic courts during or after a war, and often favour summary execution for their enemies and impunity for their allies. Proper referral to the ICC is similarly politicized. Many states, especially Great Powers like China, Russia and the USA, have opted out of the ICC, and can veto ICC referrals at the UN Security Council. Other states have these Great Powers as allies to block legal process from making headway in the ICC. This means that IHL is as weak in legal enforcement as it is elaborate in legal detail. This explains how billions of people round the world endure the routine cognitive dissonance of watching media reports of civilian massacres, torture in detention and sexual violence in war, while simultaneously being told that there are laws of war to stop them.

The lack of regular legal enforcement and explanatory court judgements in a highly legalized sphere of human activity leads inevitably to the third problem in the hyperlegalism of twenty-first-century war: self-interested interpretation and manipulation of that law. Many governments and armed groups seem to think: 'If the law is weak and untested in places then we can push our own interpretation and use IHL strategically and tactically to help us win.' Instead of merely being the arbiter of war, the law itself is viewed by states and armed groups as a useful 'weapon of war' to be exploited in a strategy cleverly labelled 'lawfare' by General Charles Dunlap, a senior US military lawyer.

One version of lawfare is to interpret the laws of war in ways that suit your interests best, as when the USA coined a new legal term to describe Al Qaeda fighters as 'illegal combatants' to deliberately put them beyond the protection of IHL and deny them prisoner of war status in Guantanamo. Lawfare also offers tactical advantages when your enemy's following of the rules of war gives you cover against an attack. The classic example here is the Taliban's tactic of breaking the law by hiding and storing military equipment in schools and mosques, well aware that law-abiding and media conscious NATO forces will avoid destroying the equipment while it is there. [40] Perhaps the most persistent example of lawfare is the fervent embrace of IHL by many governments who prefer to call a terrorist problem an 'armed conflict' so that their response to terrorists can be fully militarized and governed by the more permissive legal regime of IHL, which tolerates high levels of force, killing and destruction. This 'conflict' framing enables states to use the full force of their armed forces to kill according to the Geneva Conventions rather than the much more restrictive legal regime of human rights law.

The laws themselves are deliberately vague in key areas, having been negotiated by states and their military leaders who want to retain the right to fight hard and win. For example, IHL's key principles of proportionality and military necessity are discretionary principles to be interpreted in context, not precise rules. What exactly constitutes a proportionate response? What is military necessity? How many civilians, enemy forces and buildings can be reasonably killed and destroyed in an attack or defence? Warring parties will always bend the law towards their advantage. They will lean towards restraint in a hearts-and-minds war, and overwhelming force in an existential war. Today, targeting by Western forces cares about individual civilians and particular buildings in their calculations of proportion and necessity. They have a microscopic concern for the protection of civilians and their own forces. If geopolitical big war becomes the norm again, then different interpretations of threat and necessity may produce justifications of a legal right to kill tens of thousands of civilians and military personnel and destroy whole cities. Such is the elasticity of two of IHL's main legal principles. This makes it extremely important that all states continue to work across the widening geopolitical divides in the world today to agree humanitarian limits to their military conduct in the event of big war.

10. Public Participation in War

War this century is communicated as never before. Digital news media and mass social media have dramatically changed the way war is relayed and experienced. Militarily embedded war reporters and photographers, and specialists reporting from human rights and humanitarian agencies, are still central, but they have been joined by a mass of individuals living within war as civilians, combatants and activists.

Millions of people are using their social media accounts to visualize war, record its events, describe their experience and campaign around it. Many observers of war in countries far away have now become near real-time spectators who encounter war as remote consumers and partisan camp followers on Facebook, Twitter, Instagram and TikTok. In the 11-day war between Hamas and Israel in May 2021, the hashtag #GazaUnderAttack was used over four million times. Watching war and entering its information space by forwarding, liking and commenting on war is now routine while eating a sandwich lunch or having an evening drink in a bar thousands of miles away. The opportunity to be virtually in war or at war, wherever we are, is only a click away in our pockets, handbags and rucksacks. This is the digital era's mass version of the old picnic parties of Dunant's day when spectators in nineteenth-century Europe would lunch together while watching a battle from high ground. Like those picnics, our new information space of war is thick with information, propaganda, misinformation, disinformation, hate speech and verbal violence, alongside humanitarian appeals and calls for peace.

Military forces and armed groups all have sophisticated PR and communications divisions that are busy online designing what today's spectators are seeing, and deciding the 'truths' and narratives they absorb while they watch. In 2014, the Islamic State group launched a hashtag #AllEyesOnISIS to accompany its invasion of Iraq which rapidly became the top trending hashtag on Arabic Twitter. Its images of fierce ISIS (Islamic State of Iraq and Syria) warriors, their triumphs and atrocities, soon terrified Mosul's defending garrison, many of whom began to desert their positions.[41] Like propaganda and rumour in war from time immemorial, these new digital platforms shape the fight in the information space and on the battlefield. All major states and armed groups are now 'weaponizing' social media and engaging global audiences well beyond the conflict zone. Much of their messaging is deliberate disinformation that aims to deflect the truth, blame others and undermine their enemy. Their aim is to get their version of events to quickly go 'viral', 'sticking' in virtual space for a long time. Virtual information battles are, therefore, an intense and highly strategic area of war today.

Professor Andrew Hoskins has described how our personal digital world can be full of war if we choose. Public digital battle space is a 'global, although uneven, participative arena of fighting, commentating and experiencing' as different parties to war lay siege to popular attention and pressure people to their side in the fight. Importantly, he notes that new mass actions of 'digital outrage' at war's inhumanity have no greater effect in increasing compassion and restraint in war than the grainy photographs and prime-time TV footage of earlier ages. It seems 'the outrage society oddly numbs itself' with impassioned 'likes' and quote-tweets of violent photos, which are performed as proxies for a real effect.[42] Some in the global public may be more aware of war's detail and feel part of war in a more immediate way, but their digital engagement has not proved a magic bullet toward greater respect for humanitarian norms.

These ten characteristics of warfare have shaped the experience of war for armed forces, civilians and humanitarians over the first twenty-one years of our century. They have made up the normal operational setting of war, civilian survival and humanitarian response, but a new normal is just around the corner.

2

Next-Generation Warfare

If we now have a picture of early twenty-first-century warfare, we need to look next at what new kind of warfare is coming rapidly towards us. Today's patterns of warfare will continue in places old and new. But the scale, stakes, space and technology of war will change significantly in the next ten years as computerized warfare gathers pace and if Great Power competition turns to direct military contest. Looking ahead, I see three significant trends: the possibility of big war spread across new domains; intense computerized warfare with its distinct ethical challenges around AI; and warfare fought out in the context of deep interlocking megatrends like climate change, urbanization and increasing infectious disease.

Big War

The biggest change from the last thirty years is the new possibility of giant peer-to-peer clashes between Great Powers. New US policy in 2018 affirmed that the War on

Terror is largely over and the number-one security threat for the 2020s is 'the re-emergence of long-term, strategic competition' from China and Russia.[1] China's policy takes the same view that 'international strategic competition is on the rise… and international security is undermined by growing hegemonism, power politics, unilateralism and constant regional conflicts.'[2] Russian policy also emphasizes that the global arena is more contested. Russia's new 2021 national security strategy drops previous policies of alliance with the USA and Europe and is determined that Russia play a unique role in the world to ensure a good quality of life for its people and actively protect Russian cultural values against Westernization.[3]

The prospect of big peer-to-peer war between an increasing number of global and regional powers is making the majority of governments prepare for war with new doctrines, new battle spaces, new weapons development and new arms procurement. How they are preparing tells us what we can expect. If Great Powers and regional powers think they are fighting conventional peer-to-peer wars of survival, with no strategic incentives to respect the laws of war, then we can expect big wars in the twenty-first century to be less lawful and more awful once again. Or, equally lawful but more awful in the scale of their calculations of proportionality and military necessity that justify harming millions of people, not just hundreds of people. Either way, conventional big war would involve extremely high military and civilian casualties.[4]

This is the pessimistic reading which, not unreasonably, imagines war in this new century in the terrible image of the last century. But it may not be so. The military and humanitarian restraint of the century so far may persist. International society's equally enduring tendency to peace and cooperation around shared interests may well counter the human tendency to war. Time and politics will tell. In the meantime, it is important to spell out the military developments in the making as states prepare for big war alongside continuing sub-threshold and counter-insurgency war.

Most obvious is the accelerating arms race for military advantage. This is a 'high-end' race between rich states that are investing billions of dollars to militarily dominate new global commons, like digital space, information space and outer space, and to increase the speed, stealth and range of weapons as global military access is increasingly denied by peers. This is a race to achieve a strategic edge that could deter and overpower the enemy without formally fighting them in a major confrontation—Sun Tzu's ancient art of winning a war while avoiding a battle. All the time that states race, they fear a technological breakthrough by a rival, which would take years to catch up with and leave them intrinsically weaker for the foreseeable future.

Readiness for big war is deemed essential in the renewed contest between the Great Powers and regional powers of the twenty-first century, each of which must project power convincingly to defend their spheres of influence, secure their interests and keep a favourable balance of power in a continuously changing world. Paradoxically, strategic success in maintaining peace comes from being intensely focused on war. States must be able to win an existential war if necessary, and to show enough warlike intention and military capacity to deter their opponents by making war too costly for them.

The redistribution of global power from West to East in twenty-first-century international society has not yet found a sustainable way of balancing power and avoiding war. Commerce and trade came close to 'coupling' the USA and China, but decoupling in certain areas began again in 2016, and earlier between the West and Russia. The deterioration in regional tensions between NATO and Russia in Eastern Europe, between Saudi Arabia, Israel and Iran in West Asia, and between the USA, India, Pakistan and China in the Indo-Pacific means the threat of big war is pressing but not inevitable. But many people are already designing big war for a twenty-first-century context.

New Doctrines, Domains and Battle Spaces

Military strategists are busy shaping new doctrines for new weapons and are conceiving battle space in a new way. The first shift in big-war thinking is an expansion of the 'domains' of war—the various spaces in which battle is joined. War moved into the air last century after millennia of being fought on land and water. This century, war is being explicitly expanded into three new domains, comprising the new global commons of our age: outer space; cyber space; and information space. The Arctic is becoming a fourth new domain as the Russian government's 2021 national security strategy shows its firm intent to protect and develop its 'High North'. Climate change makes the Arctic highly strategic as a rapidly changing global space as the area warms up in the next ten years.[5] Alongside these external battle spaces, the internal domain of the human mind continues to be a highly strategic and war-winning space. New levels of digital connectivity make the minds and emotions of billions of people instantly available to information, propaganda, misinformation and disinformation, which can be used to mobilize and motivate combatants and civilians one way or the other. All these domains dramatically extend the potential 'surface' of war across new parts of Planet Earth, outer space, cyber space, our personal digital space and our individual minds.

The new domains of warfare are now routine in most military doctrine, which expects war to be fought simultaneously across all battle spaces as 'multi-domain' warfare. Military units, wherever they are, will fight using 'mosaic warfare', which will put weapons from each domain at their fingertips. New US doctrine assumes 'the end of battlefields' and the rise of 'no lines' warfare, which would 'bring fires from all domains, including space and cyber,

kinetic and non-kinetic… seamlessly'.[6] These domains—
land, sea, air, outer space, cyber space and information
space—are just the geography of war. Behind them is the
financing, weapon design, manufacture, supply, logistics
and training that make fighting possible and optimal in
every space. To read these doctrines is to have a sense of
war becoming an extremely accelerated game of six-
dimensional chess.

Access to each domain is key. The ability to fight and win
in a domain is dependent on the ability to get inside it. This
makes area access and access denial (A2/AD) a major
strategic concern for every military and a fundamental
premise of success in war. Focus on A2/AD explains China's
desire to edge the US navy and its bases out of the South
China Sea, just as it is also explains US determination to
keep China out of its 5G network and the efforts of liberal
democracies to keep Russia's cyber teams out of their
elections. It also explains the race to be well positioned in
outer space and the intense competition to develop
hypersonic glide missiles (HGM). These can leap-frog
several domains of war by being launched into space and
gliding to earth at Mach 5 speeds of 3,800 miles an hour in
a manoeuvrable flight path that dodges current air defences,
carrying conventional or nuclear warheads.[7] The enormous
effort being invested in stealth technology, which can render
planes, ships, vehicles and soldiers invisible, is another key
system to overcome access denial.

The militarization of outer space is developing fast. We can expect space to become an enormously strategic battle space in the next ten years as Great Powers seek what is called 'planetary advantage' and ensure their 'planetary security'.[8] Professor Daniel Deudney has predicted that 'planetary hegemony' will become a strategic aim and this will best be secured from outer space if one power, or an alliance, achieves space control. In the meantime, outer space is already a battle space. It is a major force multiplier because thousands of orbital satellites deploy communications and surveillance systems for terrestrial combat. These systems, often provided by 'keyhole satellites' the size of a bus, offer terrestrial mapping, navigation, early warning and tracking. Deudney therefore describes outer space as the 'back office' for current frontline fighting. Because of this, space is likely to become a target for attack from earth. Today's inter-ballistic missiles already fly via outer space, so that attacks are made through space and from space. These missiles could already make anti-satellite strikes (earth to space). In the next ten years, we can also expect the ability for terrestrial bombardment from weapons platforms in space (space to earth), and orbital or outer space combat (space to space) between such platforms.

If warfare is spreading to outer space, it will also change our most intimate human space—our bodies and our minds—in new forms of 'human enhancement'. From the earliest origins of war, warriors have taken a ritual drug, painted themselves or had a swig of rum to sharpen them up and boost their courage. In the next twenty years, human combatants will be increasingly pepped up by infotech and biotech. New pharmaceutical, digital and skeletal enhancements will increase the individual performance of combatants. Soldiers will take drugs to better manage sleep deprivation and to increase alertness and clear thinking. Digital exoskeletons connected to their neurosystem will make fighters move faster for longer—the opposite effect of body armour to date. A fighter's brain will also be increasingly fused with an array of digital information via devices that are handheld, clipped on and eventually implanted. In March 2021, Microsoft won a $22 billion contract to provide all 120,000 US close-combat soldiers with 'augmented reality headsets', which will fuse the individual soldier with images and data of what lies around the corner, over the hill and inside buildings, and allow them to send and receive real-time targeting and battle information with commanders around the globe.[9] These headsets will sense, survey, recommend, share multi-domain information, and control remote and handheld weapons. Such on-body systems announce the arrival of the multi-domain soldier and will become common across all major militaries.

Biotechnology enhancement by ingested drugs is unlikely to produce half-human 'supersoldiers' in the medium term. Like all technology, its invention, diffusion, integration and acculturation will take time. But greater human adaptation by embodied biotechnology will certainly accelerate and transform the capacity of fighters. Enhancing and automating humans poses deep ethical questions around precaution, moral autonomy and human authenticity. Major Heloise Goodley has rightly set out key ethical principles to guide these changes.[10] First, any biological changes should be agreed by individuals with informed consent and must involve 'reversible effects' so that a person is not permanently changed as sleepless, hyper alert, stronger or less afraid. Second, any biological enhancement should also leave a person's empathy and moral sense intact, and not blunt them in a way that makes them likely to be excessively and unlawfully violent or careless, or to accept and tolerate unlawful orders and immoral missions. Looking ahead, biotechnology will be as much an ethical and legal journey as computer technology.

Computerized Warfare and AI Ethics

The main part of the twenty-first-century arms race is a dash to secure advantage in new technology across all seven domains of war. This will revolutionize warfare and create forms of force and violence that we have never seen before, except in sci-fi movies: invisible weaponized spaceships; autonomous fighting robots; superhuman soldiers; and cyber attacks that use keyboards to bring states and cities to a stop in major areas of modern life.

The military benefits of greater computerization, automation, autonomy and AI are the same as they are in any other area of life. Machines are often better and cheaper for dull, repetitive, dirty and dangerous military jobs, like continuous sensing, surveillance and scenario building, or the clearance of unexploded ordinance. AI offers accelerated and expanded capacity and is a force multiplier that can operate at a much higher tempo than humans. AI-based technology can also widen the battle space and enable commanders to fight accurately 'over the horizon' (OTH). Finally, AI does not get tired or need to sleep. Nor does it have emotions, so it has no fear of death and no feelings for others. Ethically, this may give AI-based military systems 'unclouded judgement' in the heat of battle and make them more prone to honesty in reporting on their actions and their peers.[11] It also means they can be programmed to lie. The phenomenal detection skills, extreme speed, relentlessness and accuracy of AI makes it extremely valuable in surveillance and next-generation weapons. This means that AI-based war will certainly increase.

New technology rightly creates social anxiety and moral panic, whether it is the television in the 1950s, the birth control pill in the 1960s or the widespread use of the internet in the 1990s. We have a primal suspicion of our inventions that reaches back to Zeus' fury with Prometheus for giving us fire, and to Mary Shelley's modern parable of Dr Frankenstein and his autonomous monster. This is completely justified when, in nuclear weapons, we have already invented and deployed a cataclysmic war technology. AI-based weapons have the potential to be world-ending too, but there are some reasons not to panic about their eventual application and to think they may not be totally disastrous.

The main worry about computerized warfare is robot anxiety. Our computerized age of human–machine interaction poses a legitimate fear that AI, and its ability to morph beyond our expectations by 'machine learning' and 'machine-to-machine communication' (M2M), will create autonomous machines that escape our control, and even turn against us. This may happen but, equally, it may not, because we are much more adapted and resistant to machine interaction than we think.

War is traditionally made by human–machine interaction. Humans have always fused themselves with technology to enhance their strength and advantage in war ever since we first sharpened a flint and attached it to a pole to make a spear that we could carry, throw or thrust. Or, when the Mongols invented a special stirrup and merged themselves with horses in a faster and more lethal method of cavalry warfare that eventually transitioned into tanks. On water, we have combined ourselves with boats and ships, and adapted to underwater life in submarines. In the air we merged with aeroplanes, parachutes and helicopters. Soldiers routinely carry or operate automatic weapons, artillery, rockets and guided missiles. For decades we have protected ourselves with radar and communicated with electromagnetic signals that we cannot see and which most of us do not understand.

But in the early twenty-first century, as in Dunant's day, military technology stands at a profound tipping point. Human–machine interaction is increasingly human–computer interaction. This means humans designing and merging with thousands of computerized systems and sub-systems in a way that is profoundly different and extremely elaborate. With programmed algorithms as the main form of instruction to these systems, it also risks delegating extraordinary power to algorithms themselves and to those few people who design them, usually in their own image and bias, and in pursuit of their own interests.

Our robot anxiety correctly intuits that, for the first time in human history, we may be about to lose our fundamental distinction between a weapon and a warrior. This enduring distinction holds that a weapon is a material object and that a combatant is a human subject who controls the inanimate weapon. When the warrior puts down her sword or gun, it sits idle with no life of its own and unable to hurt. Conventionally, a weapon is operated by the human mind and body in conscious synthesis. Without our mind and body to operate it, the weapon is nothing.

AI-based weapons are different. Highly automated weapons with high levels of autonomy are operated by delegated algorithms that introduce significant ambiguity into the distinction between an inanimate weapon and its human operator. Many new weapons may simply continue to be weapons fashioned and variously programmed and controlled by human combatants. Or, they could change from being weapons and become non-human combatants who learn within the fight and make their own real-time decisions about killing and sparing people in war. This is already happening. Comparing past weapons with modern AI-based weapons, Professor Kenneth Payne rightly makes a key distinction: 'they were tools, whereas AI is an agent'.[12] This shift makes some scholars predict deep changes in the ontology of war because its very being, and the centre of its fighting, will move away from humans to machines. A few people see this optimistically and expect war to become less violent when it is largely fought by carefully programmed machines fighting one another. They expect more sparks to fly than blood to spurt, and they anticipate war becoming more ethical as a result.[13] I think they are overly optimistic. Computerized autonomous warfare has three key dimensions that pose deep challenges for ethics and law: machine speed; decision-making in human–machine teaming; and accountability.

As we invent increasingly fast and functionally autonomous warfare systems, and they then reinvent themselves to some degree by learning on the job, we will not be able to keep up with what they are doing. We will simply be outstripped by their sensing, speed and complexity and fail to predict, detect and control the extremely rapid actions that they take, especially if we become reliant on millions of them. This acceleration raises important questions about human–machine teaming in war. How will military people stay effectively teamed-up in real-time with millions of systems and sub-systems operating in rapid reaction to their machine peers? A commander's oversight is always prone to fog in war, but the multiplicity of machines and their superhuman speed may render human oversight impossible and make real-time command a preserve of machines not humans. Then there is the important matter of machine morality. Will human programmers be willing and able to bake in the necessary 'ethical settings' and precautions into AI systems so that they function and learn as ethical and law-based operators? Finally, if machines are acting as genuine agents, making their own decisions, do they somehow share moral responsibility with us now? Who is responsible for the firing decisions of a highly automated machine that acts in battle with functional autonomy and decision-making agency?

Human Control?

These moral risks around speed, human–machine teaming, and accountability shape today's anxiety that war will escape from human control. The problem of human control in war is not a new phenomenon, but it has never been potentially so elaborate. Archers, artillery, early aerial bombers and riflemen could never really control and predict the direction of their shot, or who might suddenly walk across the line of fire once they had taken the shot. Many weapons today, and in history, operate as much beyond human control as within it. The idea of 'reasonable precaution' has, therefore, always been used to mitigate the chronic lack of human control in war. Did the archer and the bomber try as hard as they could to judge the wind, speed and range? Did the bombers target their bombs carefully, or kick the last ones out hurriedly under heavy fire to return home fast?

Can military personnel 'stay in the loop' and hold on to some level of reasonable human control over our new AI-based weapons? Without human control, some people predict a terrible future of dystopian war. However, human control is itself quite capable of creating dystopia. Jewish people in concentration camps, people under Allied bombing in German and Japanese cities, families watching barrel bombs fall on their homes in Syria, or people starving in Somalia in 2011 all lived and died in dystopian times *because of* human control in war. Therefore, we should not romanticize human control. The bigger moral problem around human control in history so far is not that we might lose it but how intentionally awful it can be when we have it. Much human control in war is deliberately dreadful, not just accidentally so.

The longstanding problem of wicked human control in war and our continuous effort to find an ethical balance in our human–machine interactions tell us two things: that war's past was already largely dystopian anyway, and that war's future may not be worse and could even be made better by AI and new weapons that could offer more morally exacting choices to commanders. Precision weapons have certainly proved this true this century, in which the warfare of Western democracies has been much less brutal and indiscriminate than usual. If machine agency might actually have more *humanitarian* control than *human* control, it could be a desirable addition to war. A revolution in warfare and weapons is not necessarily a less ethical and more dystopian shift. It is our common responsibility to develop distinct ethics and norms around our new machines and so update the ethics of war in a way that avoids both wicked human control and wicked machine autonomy.

Cultivating Warbot Ethics

The arrival of AI's non-human intelligence in war makes it extremely important that we upgrade the ethics of war. To do this, we need to understand the kind of artificial intelligence we are shaping and the timeframe that we have to adapt our ethics and agree new rules. In his book on warbots, Professor Kenneth Payne brings an important sense of reality to the current challenge of AI-based warfare.[14] He describes how AI is 'stunningly fast' and superb at pattern recognition, which makes it brilliant at 'finding needles in haystacks'. However, 'the gap between AI and human intelligence remains profound' and warbots have a very 'limited intelligence', and this is likely to remain the case well into this century. [15] Still, experts at DeepMind are confident that their new MuZero is a first step in an AI system that can handle changing context as well as a fixed task. DeepMind's David Silver thinks human intelligence is essentially computational and so expects AI eventually to equate to human intelligence. [16] Time will tell if his idea of human intelligence is right, and his prediction correct.

AI intelligence at the moment is 'narrow' and can only focus on a specific task. It is also very 'brittle' because it fails when the task, or the conditions around it, change. AI cannot suddenly turn its attention to a completely different task. Humans can. AI also lacks key areas of human intelligence like emotion, creativity, intuition, instinct and morality. Significantly, Payne shows how AI is currently good at tactics but not strategy and concept. AI can play, dodge and weave in a specific game, and recommend the best tactical moves to win. But AI cannot do strategy or come up with an overall concept for war and victory. These require profound appreciation of political goals, insight into allies and opponents, appraisal of the possible, and winning strokes of imagination. The important differences between AI and human intelligence suggest that AI-based warfare may soon become extremely fast across all domains with functionally autonomous warbots dominating at the tactical level. But human intelligence will still dominate conceptually, strategically and emotionally, because it alone can understand that it is 'at war' and also appreciate peace; and only human intelligence can simultaneously assess why it wants to win and how it intends to do so militarily, socially, economically, politically and ethically.

So, how long have we got to shape a new AI ethics? How quickly will AI and computerized warfare dominate military activities and outstrip the speed of human thinking? In most major militaries its grip is completely mainstreamed already. Many forces would really struggle to fight 'manually' today if their computer systems were cut. They are also rebalancing their forces by building new cyber warfare forces, and the profile of a typical military person today is as much computer operator as physical fighter. Technical development and force reconfiguration will be a gradual evolution over years because absorbing and integrating AI systems into military culture and institutions requires adaptations in technique, psychology, skills and bureaucracy. But we must also expect sudden leaps in weapons developments and use in the same way as we have just had sudden vaccine leaps. These will leave ethics and law playing a desperate catch-up as increasingly autonomous military machines operate beyond the complete understanding and control of commanders, politicians and publics. This is also inevitable because most game-changing AI-based weapons systems will be developed secretly beyond public deliberation.

Gradualism rather than revolution in weapons development is ethically better because it gives more slow time for technology and morality to evolve together, and for society to invent new ethical norms around new weapons. Realistically, however, new technology always arrives as a partial mystery in human society, and its ethical and legal integration is a slow second. For example, the car became suddenly and widely used because of its many positive benefits before society realized how many people it would kill in accidents and drunk driving, and how much it would pollute the environment. People could set some early ethical rules for driving at the time of its mass take-up, but deeper ethical guidance around speed, breathalysers, seatbelts, airbags, congestion, unleaded fuel and electrification took many years. Ethically and legally, we have to understand how new technology pans out in reality before we can agree good norms and laws around it. Not everything can be foreseen in precautionary measures and bans, and it is impossible for a new technology to 'do no harm'.

Many ethicists and engineers are working hard to cultivate a new field of AI and robot ethics to guide our relationship with the new non-human intelligence of highly automated and functionally autonomous systems. Humanitarians are rightly joining in this new community, and AI ethics is now the major challenge in military and humanitarian ethics. With the arrival of warbots, their efforts are focusing on regulating the 'algorithms of violence' that will increasingly control many new weapons.[17] Warbot ethicists rightly worry about three key aspects of algorithmic killing: judgement; responsibility; and a loss of human authenticity.[18]

Judgement problems in warbots turn on hard choices that are thrown up beyond their normal activity and where the laws of war are vague. Programming war machines to target and fire carefully with functional autonomy in clear fields of fire is already relatively simple. But operational problems of distinction and proportionality in fast-moving densely populated fighting pose the same problems for warbots as they do for human combatants in the fog and friction of battle. For example, if a battle develops badly for one side and it becomes necessary to attack or defend new areas, highly automated machines will need to judge military necessity against civilian casualties and levels of destruction in their calculations of 'proportionate force' if they are fighting a humane war. How can ethical settings for proportionality be pre-set? Will human operators be able to keep pace when multiple machines are in play and using M2M learning at speed to reappraise the battle space? Humans could make these decisions and re-orientate their machines accordingly, but slowing down to do so could lose military advantage. Machines may simply be much quicker at processing the relevant information in real-time and, between them, at achieving a wider view of the battle more quickly than human commanders.

Not all moral difficulty is informational—about knowing enough in time to clarify which decision is legal and right. Some problems are simply hard to call for humans, even when they have all the information in time. What if a largely autonomous warbot has to make a sudden judgement call in a morally ambiguous situation? Perhaps it is hit by enemy fire, begins to lose control and has a choice of crashing into a school or a supermarket on a busy weekday morning. Hitting the school would mean killing predominantly children and teachers. Hitting the supermarket would mean killing more adults and pre-school toddlers and destroying essential civilian food stocks. How does it make such a decision? If the warbot defaults to a human operator at such a moment, it is likely to encounter profound moral uncertainty, even moral paralysis, in the human operator too because this is a horrendous moral choice. Should the machine, instead, be given a default ethical setting for extreme scenarios? Maybe, something like: Always prioritize the protection of children and schools. If so, who should set that ethical default command and affirm a moral preference to hit a busy supermarket instead of a busy school? Should it be the warbot's designer, engineer or operator, or the unit's commanding officer? Or should emergency default settings be agreed by parliamentary committees and defence ministries?

Problems of real-time judgement like these extend our own intrinsic moral difficulties into the realm of violent algorithms and functionally autonomous machines. These are old human dilemmas in a new format. But the question of machine accountability presents a genuinely new problem for our ideas of moral and legal accountability: Who should be accountable for a machine acting badly if that machine has high levels of functional autonomy and machine learning? What if an intelligence warbot gathers incorrect data on traffic movement, which leads to a wedding being bombed instead of an anticipated gathering of enemy commanders? Or, if a squadron of aerial attack drones makes an extreme interpretation of proportionality and bombs a neighbourhood intensely, destroying 150 homes and killing 400 civilians, while it decimates a battalion of 500 soldiers and artillery that were moving forward to take up a threatening position? These are pre-existing human problems but with a new agent—a warbot—making the decisions.

If the cause of such decisions is mechanical failure or a fundamental design flaw, then we are in familiar territory and people would look for liability and accountability with the designers and manufacturers, as has occasionally been the case with aircraft manufacturers found responsible for plane crashes. If instead these incidents are the result of functionally autonomous machines using AI to learn new information in the fight and make their own situational decisions, then we might need to think differently about moral and legal accountability. This brings us to the second concern that ethicists have concerning algorithmic killing: responsibility. Is it fair to insist that designers, manufacturers and programmers take ultimate operational responsibility for a machine that learns and has been deliberately designed to have functional autonomy in a particular setting? Some ethicists want to break new ground here. They think it best if we prepare ourselves to recognize machine agency as distinct from human agency and so distribute blame between humans and machines in a new shared form of 'hybrid liability'. This would accept that there is no hierarchical and ultimate responsibility in AI-based human–machine teaming but rather a 'network of responsibility' that includes the machine itself in familiar legal ideas of collective responsibility or joint enterprise.[19]

This is striking new moral thinking. It gives machines moral and legal personality as 'artificial moral agents' (AMA) that have 'functional morality' because they can and do make choices. This feels bizarre but is not necessarily unreasonable. It will not put a machine in the dock at the ICC in The Hague, or not yet anyway. But it would recognize the significance of machine agency and its role in mitigating the responsibility of human designers, engineers and operators because of unforeseen consequences in machines' functional autonomy to sense, target, fire or self-destruct according to their own intelligence. This view of shared human–computer responsibility is anathema to most humanitarians. They believe that humans should be kept firmly 'in the loop' throughout military operations so that human commanders have complete legal responsibility and operational control over targeting and firing by all machines, and the ability to intervene and override them at all times.

I doubt this 'in the loop' humanitarian position will hold with military reality or moral sense beyond the medium term, because AI systems will soon have a greater critical mass of high-speed operational decision-making than their human controllers. We will, therefore, be forced to conceive new ways to morally and legally regulate human–computer teaming with functionally autonomous and actively learning machines. Shared moral responsibility in human and non-human teaming is not unprecedented. The human–AI relationship may end up close to human–animal interactions in which, despite training and human control, a dog owner must still sometimes realize that their dog acted out of character and beyond human anticipation when it attacked and seriously injured a child. Both the owner and the dog share responsibility but not in equal measure. The owner is fined and prevented from owning another dog, their ultimate responsibility considered mitigated by non-human action, and the dog is killed as being primarily responsible. The same is true of storm damage and insurance liability. In matters of nature, like weather and animals, we are already used to recognizing non-human responsibility. We may soon become so in matters of non-human machines.

The third major concern of robot ethics is that increasing automation and functional autonomy in the machine world will reduce human authenticity in war. This is the worry that, as machines become more human-like and do more things that we have traditionally done, which define us somehow, like working, making, caring and fighting, then actual human life will be greatly diminished. We will have delegated to machines much that makes us human. Then, what is left of us? In war, the increase in remote and delegated killing is the touch point here because people rightly feel that war is a deeply serious matter that is trivialized if we delegate it to machines. This view holds that the moral gravity of killing and destroying in war is only properly felt and understood if we do it face-to-face and take full responsibility for our violence. Some people feel there is something deeply dishonourable about not doing the fighting ourselves and that it creates moral hazard by making war seem a cheap and easy thing to do because we no longer feel its fear, see its destruction, hear its cries and smell its corpses.

No doubt a particular warrior tradition, which valorizes bodily combat as quintessentially noble, fuels this view and deems it unworthy to sit at a computer, sipping a cup of coffee while you kill people by pressing buttons. This is similar to a person who is determined to wash their own dishes or car and avoid automatic washing machines, while most of us have become completely accustomed to machines doing it for us. Kant might agree and say the most significant element of ethics is in our intention: the intent to have a clean car or to kill within ethical limits is the key thing. How we do them matters less. But perhaps war is different and human process is more important when killing is at stake. Many people certainly do sense the moral hazard in machine-fighting. Will new technology make light of war, as something more imaginary than real, more a screen-based than scream-based activity? Will people pause to ask, 'What have we done?' if they have not done it and were not really there? Remote killing is obviously not stress-free. Drone pilots show and report significant combat stress and moral uncertainty when they are destroying people and places remotely from another country; but this is still quite intimate human–machine teaming with the human in control. It is hard to know what will happen to war's personal moral weight when AI systems do more and more in war, and when killing and harming are played out on screen in much more delegated teaming with decisions far too fast for humans to try to understand. I expect there will inevitably be a difference, but we will still feel it and weigh it heavily when people are doing their best to hurt us back in the same way. The currency will be different but the suffering will have the same value in a largely computerized war.

There is one area where the moral remoteness of machine war seems particularly alarming: the deliberate perpetration of massacre and genocide. Studies of genocides all show two key steps in a numbing process that enables one group to wipe out another. The first step is to de-humanize the enemy and render them sub-human to the feelings and imagination of those who must kill them. The second is to bureaucratize the process so that many people who organize genocide— listing, finding, gathering, transporting—are able to do it as a series of discrete bureaucratic tasks without knowledge of the final outcome or a sense of any direct part they have played in it. So the person who draws up the lists or drives the trucks does not know why they are doing it or where the people are going in the end. These two steps of sensory and bureaucratic distancing will be extremely easy to achieve if machines are managing most, or all, of the process from selection to eradication. Equally terrible and morally remote would be the delegation of torture to machines.

Warfare in an Era of Climate Crisis and Disease

Today's arms race is primarily generated by a view of security and defence that concentrates on Great Power rivalry, global influence and military threat. But climate crisis and the global rise in infectious diseases are also driving security thinking and military calculation. In twenty-first-century security policy, environment and disease are not only difficult things that militaries have to control when fighting a war; they are also becoming possible reasons for going to war. Alarmingly, climate and disease may be changing from being *conditions* of warfare to *causes* of war.

Warfare has always been carried out in some of the world's extreme environments, like deserts, jungles, swamps and snow, which have produced military specialisms as a result. Warfare has also routinely destroyed and polluted the natural environment, which has rightly made the protection of the environment a central priority in the laws of war alongside civilian protection.[20] Similarly, throughout military history, infectious disease has been a constant factor in warfare, too, as soldiers have died from diseases in large numbers, often determining victory or defeat. Military forces have also acted as super-spreaders: most catastrophically as European Conquistadores in the Americas, but elsewhere, too, with sexually transmitted diseases, typhus, Spanish Flu and HIV. Throughout military history, therefore, disease and climate have been conditions to be well managed by armed forces to keep them fighting at full tempo. But extremes of climate and disease are about to get much worse, with significant military consequences.

In the next ten years, climate crisis will transform military forces by shaping how and where they locate their forces and how they fight. Pressing climate threats mean the world's largest military forces must adapt their assets and warfighting methods fast. Hundreds of expensive and sophisticated military bases around the world are directly threatened by rising sea levels, floods, fire and extreme heat. They will have to be relocated, as the most immediate threat to many naval bases, airfields and army camps are now environmental hazards not enemy attack. Billions of dollars of military equipment and hundreds of thousands of military personnel are at risk from sudden flooding, raging fires, melting runways and overheating machines. This means that climate-safe locations will become a major priority for all military forces and that we can expect a major geographical reconfiguration of the world's military forces and footprint as they move to new areas or mitigate and adapt existing locations. But climate change not only threatens military installations and personnel: it will also dramatically change two other things for the world's military forces—their operational environment and their energy use.

Twenty-first-century militaries will routinely be required to fight in extremely hostile climates. Armed forces will need to fight and move in rising temperatures, and in increasingly dry zones and increasingly wet zones, as centres of production and population change. A struggle for the Arctic would involve sustained operations in snow and ice. Warfare in outer space and zero gravity will be extremely challenging to human forces. Extreme weather conditions and outer space are likely to make more resilient warbots the weapon of choice over more fragile human formations, and climate change will accelerate the shift to robotic warfare.

Human military formations must also adapt to dramatic climate hazards while campaigning. Sudden floods, fires, freezes and heatwaves will become as routine as threats from enemy action. Indeed, fires and floods may be deliberately manipulated as part of enemy action. Luring one's enemy onto a floodplain or near a forest prone to fire may be the best way to wipe them out. There is a long tradition of using nature to destroy one's enemy, as Napoleon discovered when his army was decimated by the freezing Russian winter. Instrumentalizing climate hazards will become a major military art during the climate crisis. New clothes, vehicles, equipment, military formations, strategies, tactics, logistics and methods will be needed for warfare as militaries adapt quickly to climate change in the next ten years. Not all this next-generation warfare will be happening in the wilds of a newly hazardous nature. Global population is largely urban and increasingly urban. Towns, cities and informal settlements will continue to be where most people meet the climate crisis head-on. People are now regularly migrating to cities to escape failed agricultural landscapes and may soon also be migrating from failing cities as sea levels and temperatures rise to unmanageable degrees. This means that warfare and violence will remain deeply urban except where contests open up over newly available global commons like the Arctic and outer space.

Energy transition is another climate-related factor that will transform military forces. The world's large militaries are some of the biggest producers of carbon emissions in the world, and many of them are already highly focused on achieving an energy transition to reach net zero in the next twenty years. As part of its Costs of War programme, the

Watson Institute has examined the climate costs of war. They estimated that between 2001 and 2019 American military involvement in the Global War on Terror produced 1.2 billion metric tonnes of greenhouse gases. More than 400 million tonnes were due to war-related fuel consumption.[21] In the UK, the Ministry of Defence is responsible for half of all UK government emissions. British forces are already switching to 'hybrid fuels' for planes and ships, which mix carbon and renewables. Like US forces, they are setting clear targets for energy transition.[22] Moving to renewables has clear strategic benefits, too. Large logistics operations to supply carbon-based fuel are very expensive and highly vulnerable to attack. Switching may be cheaper in blood and treasure (i.e. lives and money), while also offering significant strategic advantage. Alternative energy sources can create more agile military forces that are lighter on their feet and in their installations and supply. Today's military strategists expect energy transition to increase operational resilience and flexibility.

Infectious diseases also pose a major threat to modern military capabilities. Changing climate is creating a new global geography of disease as dengue, malaria and other vector-borne diseases spread out to new areas of the globe and re-infect zones where they were previously eradicated. New zoonotic epidemics like Ebola and COVID, and increasing resistance to antibiotics, will make campaigning military forces extremely vulnerable to disease threats.

Before the invention of vaccination and antibiotics, it was common for armies to be devastated by disease rather than by the enemy. Military campaigns were won and lost because of infection just as often as by feats of arms. This risk in warfare is returning, and medical adaptation will once again become a major military priority if human forces are to be maintained at strength and expensive investments in military training are not to be rendered useless in a moment by microbial attack. Military public health will become increasingly strategic once again. In the century so far, war surgery has been the innovative edge of military medicine, with astonishing progress in medevac, 'golden hour' management, field surgery and rehabilitation. Public health management of infectious disease and extreme environments now looks set to return as a major challenge to military medicine and military capability.

The Rise of Non-traditional Security Threats

Extreme climate hazards and disease are not only challenging conditions to be mitigated and managed when fighting a war: they may soon become the reasons for a war. The risk of climate wars and health wars has long been anticipated in the field of non-traditional security (NTS). Thinking about NTS has emerged strongly in East and Southeast Asia, which, in many ways, tasted the non-military threats of climate and disease before the West in the Asian financial crisis of 1997, the SARS epidemic in 2002 and the Indian Ocean Tsunami of 2004, and in recurring floods, fires, transnational air pollution and extensive migration. The West is now catching up. In 2020, the USA suffered more deaths from COVID than it did in World War II, showing how a pandemic can be a greater threat to human life than armed conflict and terrorism. Improved forecasting and civil preparedness play a key role in the management of non-traditional threats, and this is now happening fast. In January 2021, the US government set up the new National Centre for Epidemic Forecasting and Outbreak Analytics as a global early warning system to prevent, detect, respond to and recover from emerging biological threats. This complements existing US forecasting systems for extreme weather events and food security. In April 2021, the UK did the same with a new UK Health Security Agency.

Professor Mely Caballero-Anthony, a pioneer of the NTS approach, characterizes non-traditional threats as transnational, ungovernable, sudden, enormous and urgent.[23] Their scale and spread puts them beyond the power of a single government and they become challenges for regional or whole world 'governance' by expert communities of scientists, health professionals, security forces, humanitarians and development 'governors', working in wide networks of formal state and non-state organizations to avert catastrophe. The COVID pandemic has made the world well aware of this kind of non-military threat, but

COVID may be a relatively gentle rehearsal for major climate crisis and new diseases with much higher kill rates than COVID.

It is already clear that climate crisis is rapidly changing the political geography of what is valuable and what is not. Warming temperatures mean that the far north of Russia and Canada are becoming increasingly productive high-value spaces. Russia has recently become the largest wheat producer and exporter in the world as its climate opens up more to arable farming, while other agricultural zones farther south across the globe close down because of extreme heat. Canada and the UK are set to become major wine producers in the next ten years as large parts of the USA and the Mediterranean are no longer fit for grape and wine production because of drought. Some farmers in Sicily, who have abandoned grapes, are now farming tropical fruits like avocados, mangoes and lychees. Many are failing to adapt.[24] Energy transition—the shift away from carbon fuels—will also change the face of global security and political risk as areas rich in crude oil and gas greatly reduce in their political and economic significance, while zones rich in minerals and metals essential to renewables and batteries become highly strategic. In short, people are likely to compete over very different places and resources in the next ten years as new areas of the world achieve strategic climate significance.

But what if international cooperation and global governance fail to manage this new competition and adaptation fairly in everyone's interest? The role of war as a response to non-military threats is not yet openly articulated in Great Power doctrines, but military strategists are thinking that phenomena like climate change and disease may soon cause war. A US academic study of climate and conflict in 2015 seems to have influenced US security thinking. Professor Marshall Burke's team made a meta-analysis of the connection between climate change and conflict incidence, which concluded: 'adverse climatic events increase the risk of violence and conflict at both the intergroup and interpersonal level in societies around the world and throughout human history'.[25] The connection is not a direct link, e.g. that if you are hotter then you are more violent. Instead, they noted how increased temperature and rainfall produce 'multiple pathways' into conflicts over trade, natural resources, land use, rising sea levels and changing disease geographies, as well as psychological changes in people's threat perceptions and their sense of the risk and rewards of violence, which may increasingly seem a survivalist option.

In 2017, the US government took up this multiplier approach and identified six pathways down which they anticipate conflict will be 'fuelled' by climate change alone: destabilization of countries; heightened social and political tensions; food shortages and price rises; increased health risks; collapse of investment value and economic competitiveness; and sudden devastating climate surprises.

All these might cause a resort to violence in armed conflicts, rising crime, military crackdowns by governments, or popular uprisings. On taking up his new role as US Secretary of Defense in January 2021, Lloyd Austin immediately declared that the USA would now treat climate change as a national security priority. In February 2021, the UK government put climate, COVID and conflict firmly on the agenda of the UN Security Council as a dangerously interlinked trio of threats to international peace and security.

China, Russia and India have been relatively reticent so far about how they think climate, energy transition, health, urbanization, migration and other megatrends will shape global security and the use of force in the next ten years. But international lawyers are already imagining how one state's response to climate change—by water-hoarding or geostrategic engineering in space—could prompt a defensive attack by another state that feels the negative effects of a rival's climate mitigation. This would see climate action itself becoming a reason for war if one state's mitigation is another state's deprivation. The same security risks could arise from disease management and food security policies.

Sadly, it seems we can expect communities and states to use force to defend themselves militarily if they perceive climate, disease, migration and pollution as a threat to their survival. The first twenty years of the century have given us glimpses of this already in militarized push-backs and citizen attacks against migrants in South Africa, Europe,

Southeast Asia and the Americas. The survivalist dimension of these non-traditional security threats makes it understandable but regrettable that states should see them as hard security problems. The challenge today must be to leverage states' growing view of climate and disease as security threats to incentivize them to work together on climate and health multilateralism to find peaceful solutions in regional and global cooperation. Diplomacy and global governance, not war, should be the priority for solving these common challenges. But even talking about these megatrends in highly securitized language runs moral risks in how we see suffering people. In 'health security' talk, a sick person risks becoming an enemy instead of a patient. In 'food security' thinking, a hungry person may become a threat instead of a guest. In 'climate security', the climate action of a community or a state may be 'defended' like other national infrastructure.

If politicians and publics are not careful, a security framing for these challenges may lead intuitively to a military response. It is better to keep talking of climate and disease as challenges for human wellbeing and planetary protection instead of national security. The mutual wellbeing frame resonates with a challenge of cooperation rather than defence, and it calls us to find peaceful ways to solve climate crisis and disease. This huge task is one of fair and cooperative adaptation: navigating our way through a global energy transition beyond carbon fuels; protecting and sharing new patterns of rural and urban land use; creating a new, inclusive and prosperous global economy that is much less environmentally damaging while, all the time, fending off new diseases and ill health brought about by climate change. However, humans being what we are, the person who writes about twenty-first-century warfare at the end of the century may well write mostly about big 'climate wars' and 'disease wars' spurred on by contests over mitigation and adaptation. I hope not.

Part Two

CIVILIANS

The human experience of war has always been much wider than the experience of those who fight it in military forces. War today is a social and economic disaster for hundreds of millions of people who may never see or hear a battle. War makes poor people even poorer—as displaced people in unplanned settlements miles from their homes—and drives comfortable middle-class people into poverty in a matter of weeks. The next two chapters look at the civilian experience of the wider phenomenon of war, and how it destroys and reorganizes people's lives. War's violence makes people's normal lives unliveable and forces them to move to find new sources of safety, food, health and livelihood. Families are separated by military conscription, detention, flight and migration. War's violence, disruption and loss are also deeply upsetting. War breaks hearts, shatters trust, creates hatred and saddens minds.

But people are also remarkable in war. They mostly do what human beings always do, by surviving, acting and adapting. People's energy and agency are redirected to coping, caring and resisting. New forms of power and determination take shape in political and social organizations at all levels of society. It takes just five minutes in a camp of displaced people, a market in a bombed-out town square, or a classroom with no roof to realize that most people enduring war are strongly focused on carrying on, not giving up. Civilians' own agency in surviving war is impressive and needs to be respected and supported.

3

Civilian Experience

The civilian experience of war was not on Dunant's mind at Solferino, but it almost completely preoccupies his descendants in today's Red Cross and Red Crescent Movement and their humanitarian cousins in the United Nations agencies and non-governmental organizations (NGOs). Many of these, like UNICEF, WFP, OCHA, Save the Children, the International Rescue Committee, Oxfam, CARE, Lutheran World Federation, Caritas, World Vision, MSF and Islamic Relief, were founded with a civilian mission in or after subsequent wars. Today, the 'protection of civilians' (PoC) is the core policy of the humanitarian world and a permanent agenda item on the UN Security Council, where causing widespread civilian suffering is considered a threat to international peace and security, and potentially criminal too.

How much do we really know about the experience of civilians in twenty-first-century wars, their suffering and hardships, and their resilience and creativity? The answer is mixed, even in this data-driven era. This is for two reasons: data difficulties in consolidating information in the fog of war, and humanitarian hype, which can misrepresent civilian experience.

Data Fog and Humanitarian Hype

Data difficulties make it genuinely hard to get an accurate handle on the extent of civilian suffering and resilience in war, although data systems are improving fast. This is especially true about civilian deaths. Today there are several new datasets that track civilian mortality by formal 'casualty-counting' for violent civilian deaths. They use information generated close to events by official sources, community reporting, media sources and observers.[1] Most figures we have for civilian deaths are approximations, and political propaganda tends to hide or exaggerate war deaths. For example, at the end of the Bosnian war in 1996 it was widely claimed that 250,000 civilians had been killed. Eight years later, an objective scientific study estimated total war deaths at 140,000 with a 50/50 split between civilian and military deaths.[2]

Professor Keith Krause has dedicated much of his career to calculating, explaining and campaigning against the suffering from armed violence and war. He still sees violence statistics as deeply problematic because counting is always uncertain and today's different datasets count different things. He notes how media-based reporting used by most datasets tends to undercount deaths and that different parameters for including a death result in dramatically different figures. For example, in Iraq between 2003 and 2015, Iraq Body Count estimated total violent war deaths at 220,000 with up to 166,085 being civilians. The Uppsala dataset counted only 53,361 deaths in total for the period and came out so low because, strangely, their method insists on identifying a perpetrator as well as a victim to confirm and so include a violent death.[3]

Casualty-counting is a new science, spurred on by civil society efforts to monitor US wars since 2001, and by UN systems which attempt to coordinate humanitarian aid. The consolidation of civilian casualty information into global data is an important twenty-first-century innovation. But wider war deaths from poverty, hunger and disease are also hard to count. During war, hundreds of humanitarian agencies gather data on health, food supply, market prices and asset levels and are beginning to make progress in consolidating these data into national and global reporting, and to use them effectively to anticipate worsening conditions. Having humanitarian data means we can dip into numerous district studies for an indication of war's social impact and also get a general picture of areas in which hunger, displacement and disease are rising and falling.[4] We can see trends and increasingly predict deterioration and improvement, but we can seldom give reliable totals. The data we have also focus mainly on populations who are seen by humanitarians. Their gaze is often skewed towards particular groups they can reach, and in whom they are especially interested—like women, children and displaced people. These preferences leave out many others. Humanitarian data also focus almost entirely on needs and do not track and study how well people are surviving without aid.

This well-placed humanitarian emphasis on seeking out suffering, needs and vulnerable groups creates the second main obstacle to understanding civilian lives: most descriptions of civilian experience come to us from humanitarian and human rights sources, and the media. Their desire to find and emphasize the worst can exaggerate and misrepresent civilian suffering and under-report civilian survival and adaptation. Humanitarian organizations have a vested interest in talking up a crisis. A running narrative of Dunant-like 'horror' keeps them on brand and ensures humanitarian efforts receive political attention and finance. There is evident truth in many of the details that humanitarians promote, but they also encourage a pattern of misleading statistics and stereotypes which gives rise to the misrepresentation of civilian lives statistically, spatially and by gender.

Professor Kelly Greenhill has shown how humanitarians promote certain 'magical numbers', which come to operate as 'social facts' in the halls of government to drive perception, policy and finance, even though they are not actual facts.[5] These magical numbers and their humanitarian myths last a long time. For example: the long-cited figure that 2 million children were killed in conflicts in the decade from 1986 to 1996. This statistic was used to imply that these children were violently killed. The figure was given unsourced in an international aid organization's report in 1996, and repeatedly requoted across the humanitarian sector to (mis)characterize the scale of children's violent deaths in war well into the 2010s. No evidence for it was ever found. Another widely circulated magic number is that up to 90% of people killed in war today are civilians, a statistic which is usually understood, by those who read it in media statements, to mean violent battle deaths. This, too, is a mythic simplification and certainly does not hold across all wars. For example, the Syrian Observatory for Human Rights, which has made great efforts to track individual violent deaths in Syria's war, gives a total figure of 594,000 violent deaths in the first ten years of the Syrian war, from 2011 to 2021.[6] Their records show that 117,388 of these were civilian deaths and a much larger figure of 476,000 were combatants killed fighting for government forces, armed groups or as mercenaries. Equally against the grain of current humanitarian rhetoric is their count that 81,279 of the civilian deaths were adult males, some 69% of civilian violent deaths, when humanitarians typically emphasize the suffering of women and children.

Two other statistical mantras widely used by humanitarians are rightly criticized, both relating to displacement: that more people are displaced today than ever before, and that 80% of displaced people are women and children. The claim of unprecedented displacement from war is simply wrong.[7] Displacement around the globe in World War II ran into hundreds of millions of people, which was much higher in absolute terms and relative to the global population. Forced displacement in World War I was probably also higher than today as a proportion of the population. The statistic that 'two-thirds' or sometimes '80%' of internally displaced persons (IDPs) today are women and children has also been widely repeated.[8] This is a good example of a statistic that may be true in certain places but which is then globalized as a policy slogan, which shifts humanitarian programming almost entirely towards displaced women and children. A closer look at the data for 2019 reveals that 21 million IDPs were women and girls out of a global total of 41 million, so we could also say that almost 50% of IDPs are men and boys. The 'two-thirds' claim is made for Africa and the Middle East, where displaced women and girls are indeed a higher proportion in countries that disaggregate data by sex. But the same report also notes that 'only 15% of the countries on which IDMC [Internal Displacement Monitoring Centre] collects data provided information disaggregated by gender and age', which undermines the claim even for Africa and the Middle East. This IDP mantra also overlooks the fact that the majority of asylum seekers arriving in third countries from war are men, many of whom endure terrible journeys and are often detained in the process.[9]

Humanitarian rhetoric misrepresents war and civilian experience spatially, too. Agencies repeatedly use phrases like 'conflict-affected countries' and 'countries at war', or they label whole countries as 'conflict-ridden'. In the popular and political imagination of people far away, these blanket terms give a misleading impression that a whole country is at war, and that everyone in Afghanistan or Mali is exposed to the kinds of bombardment and civilian massacres we see close up in media and humanitarian reports. Countrywide generalizations are reinforced by statistics which leave the impression that billions of people are living as civilians in the middle of wars today. They are not.

For example, an influential report on children and armed conflict by the Peace Research Institute Oslo (PRIO) claimed that '1.6 billion children are living in a conflict-affected country', which is '69% of all the world's children'.[10] Having lodged this huge figure in people's minds, PRIO's report focuses on more detailed descriptions, but the overall impression is conveyed that war is everywhere and overwhelming nearly 70% of children globally. PRIO's data were used to great campaigning effect by Save the Children in their centenary report in 2019, *Stop the War on Children*,[11] but they eschewed the 1.6 billion statistic and zoomed in on PRIO's data and its narrower parameter of 'conflict zones'.

These are areas within 50 kilometres of a place with more than 25 violent battle deaths per year. But this is not a lot, and easily compares to places like Chicago where, around the 4 July weekend alone in 2021, some 100 people were shot and 18 were killed.[12] The figure now becomes 420 million children or 'one fifth of all children in the world'. Save the Children's report then uses PRIO's criteria to zoom in further and show that 142 million children are in 'high intensity conflict zones' within 50 kilometres of an area with more than 1,000 deaths per year, which is a lot. So, we have started with a headline figure of 1.6 billion children in war and finally arrived at less than one-tenth of this figure where children are living in something which most people would understand as war. This is still a very large number of children in extremely dangerous and damaged areas, but humanitarian reports might create less moral panic and better policy and financing if they got straight to the point.

This wide spatial framing of 'conflict', which is similarly routine in Red Cross, UN and World Bank rhetoric, catastrophizes whole countries in a way that is simply not accurate for most twenty-first-century wars. Professor Clionadh Raleigh analyses the 'conflict geography' of violence against civilians. She also leads ACLED, one of the new global datasets monitoring violence globally. Raleigh's evidence suggests that in armed conflicts, on average 15% of a state's territory has active violence, and that all conflicts have 'hot spots and cold zones'. Most violence against civilians today is intermittent and used by governments and armed groups to flex their power and demonstrate control in certain areas. This means most violence is 'dotted' around a particular area and flares up and down in short 'spirals'.[13] The social impact of war is similarly concentrated in displaced communities fleeing from attacks, their host communities, contested districts and urban areas under siege. Only Iraq, Syria, South Sudan and Yemen have been comprehensively affected by war, with their whole societies impoverished and transformed by violence extending across the entire surface of their territory at various times. Otherwise, in countries like Nigeria, the Democratic Republic of Congo, Mali, Cameroon, Afghanistan and Ukraine, war's violence is localized. It is not incessant, widespread and overwhelming across the whole country.

Civilian Experience in the Century So Far

Despite these difficulties of data, statistics and humanitarian hype, it is possible to build a picture of civilian suffering and survival in twenty-first-century wars to date by looking at civilian deaths, the socio-economic impact of war, the gendering of civilian experience, civilian survival and civilian attitudes to war.

Civilian Deaths

One thing we do know is that the number of civilians who have been violently killed in 'battle deaths' is strikingly low this century compared to last century. The same is true for civilian death from hunger, disease, impoverishment or inhumane treatment in detention, which statisticians call 'indirect deaths'. This is good news and is not well communicated by humanitarian and human rights professionals. The kind of wars being fought and the relatively small forces fighting them are one reason. Major investment in humanitarian response is almost certainly another, although humanitarians and their government financiers have never really checked for this.

The distinction between direct and indirect death is very important for explaining civilian deaths. Battle deaths by bullet, bomb or blade are described as 'direct' battle deaths, when civilians are killed violently in acts of war. Deaths from hunger, disease and destitution are termed 'indirect' because civilians die from war's wider social impact. Indirect deaths may be reasonably counted over a long time in an area or across a country because people die from war's effects many years later. Their health, education and economic status are permanently damaged by the war, which reduces their overall life chances. For example, we may legitimately count the many suicides of Vietnam veterans years after their return to the USA as war-related deaths. In the same way, a young girl who never went to secondary school because of war in northern Nigeria will spend her adult life hawking cigarettes in the street when she might have got a business qualification and been a manager in a medium-sized business, helping to grow her local economy. Her life chances were forever affected by war.

Unless a war involves deliberate strategies of widespread civilian massacre, like the genocides and the deliberate saturation aerial bombing of cities last century, it is assumed that more civilians die indirectly from the destitution and impoverishment of war than directly from its violence. Stanford University medical professor Paul Wise has reviewed many excess mortality studies from recent wars and concludes that most civilians die indirectly from 'the destruction of essentials' at a rate that is typically double all battle deaths.[14] Famine increases this ratio dramatically, as, for example, when 244,000 people died from war-induced famine in Somalia in 2011, a number many times higher than Somalia's battle deaths that year and the only famine in the century so far.[15] Hunger in Yemen may prove equally deadly and its mortality will significantly outweigh civilian battle deaths. Civilian death rates can also multiply in middle-income countries, like Iraq and Syria, where people have high levels of non-communicable diseases, like heart disease, cancer and diabetes. When health systems are destroyed or collapse in war, such people lose access to routine treatment and die early deaths from war's effects.

Accurate data on indirect civilian deaths are difficult to find because calculations of excess mortality from war-induced poverty, illness and hunger tend to be controversial because they use statistical modelling. But excess mortality studies are now routinely contributing to our understanding of civilian experience. In 2004, Professor Les Roberts compared mortality data in the months before and after the US invasion of Iraq, including communities around fierce fighting in Fallujah. His team estimated that the risk of death was 2.5 times greater after the invasion; that 98,000 people had died in Iraq because of war; and that the main cause of death had changed from heart disease to violence in the first nine months of US occupation.[16] A more recent study by the London School of Hygiene and Tropical Medicine of excess mortality from war in South Sudan between December 2013 and April 2018 looked at direct deaths from killing and indirect deaths. This survey found links between increased mortality and conflict intensity, displacement, food security, reduced vaccination and cholera outbreaks, and estimated that 190,000 people were violently killed and 383,000 people died from war's social and economic effects in these five years.[17] This would mean an average of 114,000 people dying each year because of war in a population of around 10 million.

Fewer Civilian Battle Deaths

Accurately counting civilian battle deaths has been attempted in great detail in current US wars. A team at the Watson Institute at Brown University has been assiduously tracking direct civilian violent deaths by all sides in America's wars, using a variety of sources (see Table 3.1). In

Afghanistan, they estimate that 43,074 civilians have been violently killed by both sides between 2001 and 2019. In Iraq, the number is much more—up to 207,156 people since 2003. In Syria, civilian deaths in the US war against the Islamic State group between 2014 and 2019 (not the wider Syrian conflict) saw 49,591 people violently killed by both sides. Some 12,000 civilians have been violently killed in Yemen's war since 2002. Many civilians will also have been wounded but not killed in all these attacks, often with life-changing injuries.

These figures report on the world's militarily biggest long wars, which mix high-tech conventional warfare with insurgency, terror bombing by air and IED, and counter-insurgency methods. The Watson Institute team is very aware that its figures are a best estimate and not precision science, because all militaries often under-report civilian casualties and also tend to count men as combatants and so regularly 'blur' military and civilian categories to make themselves look better. In addition, civilians meet violent deaths in war that are not battle deaths. Many thousands of civilians are killed in detention by torture, execution and overcrowding. Many others die from their injuries weeks or months later. Civilians are also killed in acts of sexual violence, or die later from infections, wounds and despair that are the after-effects of these attacks. Current systems of counting violent civilian deaths are incomplete estimates. Nevertheless, the Watson Institute's figures give us an approximate view of civilian battle deaths this century.

Table 3.1: Direct civilian violent deaths by all sides in
America's wars

Type of battle death	Afghanistan 2001–2019	Iraq 2003–2019	Syria 2014–2019 ISg war only	Yemen 2002–2019	Total
All sides military battle deaths	129,373	96,848	171,026	99,323	496,570
All sides civilian battle deaths	46,319	208,964	95,000	12,690	362,973

Note: Extracted from Neta C. Crawford and Catherine Lutz, 'Human cost of post-9/11 wars: Direct war deaths in major war zones: Afghanistan & Pakistan Oct. 2001–Aug. 2021; Iraq March 2003–Aug. 2021; Syria Sept. 2014–May 2021; Yemen Oct. 2002–Aug. 2021, and other post-9/11 war zones', Watson Institute, Brown University, 21 September 2021, at https://watson.brown.edu/costsofwar/figures/2021/WarDeathToll

Statistics seldom make sense in isolation. Many of us have become armchair statisticians in the COVID pandemic and know we cannot weigh the gravity of COVID death rates unless we also know the rate at which people die of other things, like cancer, heart disease, HIV/AIDS, malaria or flu. So, how shall we compare and interpret the scale of direct civilian battle deaths in these conflicts? We have already seen that they are fewer than the huge numbers of civilian deaths last century, which routinely reached into the hundreds of thousands or millions in several conflicts. Perhaps there are other relevant twenty-first-century comparisons to show how people die in the world today.

First, we can compare them with military deaths to see that violent civilian deaths are considerably lower than military deaths, except in Iraq. This is already contrary to the impression we get from most humanitarian rhetoric, which emphasizes civilians. Second, we can look at the global significance of civilian battle deaths compared to other violent causes of death around the world. Civilian war deaths are sudden violent deaths at the hands of other people that are both deliberate and unintentional. This seems similar in character to homicide and road traffic accidents. The World Health Organization (WHO) estimates that 1.35 million people globally were killed in car crashes in 2019 with between 20 million and 50 million people injured. This is obviously a much higher number of deaths per year than civilian battle deaths over several years. Homicides are also much higher. The Geneva Declaration's study of all global violent deaths estimated that there were about 508,000 violent deaths each year across the world between 2007 and 2012, about 70,000 of which were violent civilian battle deaths in war each year.[18] These global comparisons are revealing. They show that direct civilian battle deaths this century are very low compared to the last century and are relatively small compared to other causes of violent death worldwide in the early twenty-first century.

These comparatively low civilian battle deaths should be reassuring to humanitarian policymakers, but this is not a message we hear from them or a message that it is easy for them to give publicly for fear of implying that higher deaths are normal. Instead, humanitarian rhetoric against civilian battle deaths is as loud as ever and military policymakers and the general public hear little sound of war's improvement from humanitarians. This may signal a deeper trend in Western humanitarian consciousness implied by intolerance of civilian casualties even when they are relatively low. Continuous humanitarian 'outrage' suggests there is an abolitionist ambition in Western humanitarianism today that finds any civilian death an aberration, and that is working towards a form of war with combatant battle deaths alone. This is a moral position that goes beyond the current laws of war in which civilian deaths in battle are permitted by military necessity so long as they are not deliberate, indiscriminate or disproportionate. Abolition is also a moral position that is likely to be deeply disappointed in any return to big war. But I may be wrong, and perhaps we are living in a new humanitarian era of war in which human society and ethics are genuinely and enduringly intolerant of any civilian battle deaths. I hope so, but I doubt it. Instead, I fear that the last thirty years of liberal order and limited Great Power competition may be a niche period of restraint between more typical times of greater acceptance of massive civilian battle deaths. If twenty-first-century humans are existentially threatened by attack and have the military power to respond, I doubt that we will prove to be more angelic than our ancestors.

The Death–Displacement Ratio

The most fundamental feature of civilian experience in twenty-first-century wars can be expressed in the death–displacement ratio rather than in violent death itself. This is a basic pattern in wars today, which shapes a great part of civilian life: relatively few violent civilian deaths in war drive exponential numbers of displacements. It is not violent death that dominates the majority civilian experience of war today, but the disruption and impoverishment of displacement as people try to avoid violent death. For example, in Yemen, the ratio of violent deaths to displacements is 1:333, in Nigeria it is 1:160, and in Mozambique's relatively recent war it already stands at 1:265.[19] War today is much more likely to affect civilians by displacing them than killing them, and it is their displacement and its resulting poverty, hunger and ill health that makes most civilians suffer.

A series of attacks, which may kill tens or hundreds of people at a time, destroy homes, farms and businesses, and damage water and electrical supplies, can cause the flight, displacement and impoverishment of millions. This is because life becomes too dangerous in the vicinity of murdering armed groups or terrorizing government forces, and unliveable when teachers, nurses, shopkeepers, bankers, engineers and government officials also flee, which they often do, and so business and public services collapse.

This extensive displacement is often the intended outcome of combatants who want to disrupt society, disperse certain populations and rearrange the political demography of the area. Such intent has been seen most starkly this century in the genocidal forced displacements of people in Darfur and the Rohingyas in Myanmar. War's violence is also made more terrifying still by particular 'signature atrocities' deployed by armed groups and governments, such as beheadings, gang rape, barrel bombing, or kidnapping. Every conflict also has its 'micro-violence', which sees old inter-group scores and personal grievances played out in violence pretending to be war. All this combined means that today's relatively small numbers of civilian deaths, compared to twentieth-century warfare, still catalyse a much wider social disaster.

War is a Socio-economic Disaster

Even if the numbers of direct and indirect deaths are contested estimates, the effects of displacement and the wider 'destruction of essentials' are clear. It is possible to describe in general terms how warfare, even when militarily small and sporadic, disrupts and destroys significant parts of society. Two different types of war today serve as sadly representative examples of how war is a social and economic disaster: the war in Syria, which started in 2011, and the war in northern Nigeria between the government of Nigeria and the Islamist armed movement called Boko Haram, which became openly violent in 2009. The Syrian war touched almost every corner of the country at some stage. The Nigerian war has stayed in one corner of northeast Nigeria but also spread disastrously across its borders into Cameroon, Niger and Chad.

Syria's war stands out this century as exceptionally deadly and intense because it has involved an entrenched repressive regime with a huge security apparatus supported by powerful international allies in Russia and Iran, fighting a nationwide rebellion of secular and Jihadist armed groups that are also supported by powerful international allies. Foreign fighters and mercenaries have also played a significant part on both sides. As a result, the war spread fast across the whole country and produced widespread destruction in several of its biggest cities, and extraordinary levels of displacement and poverty. A phenomenal 6.6 million Syrians are displaced within the country and a further 6.7 million live as refugees beyond its borders.[20] This is well over half the population, made homeless by the war. With destruction and displacement come impoverishment and destitution as people are forced to give up their assets, businesses and jobs to start again somewhere, or live off savings, loans, family charity and aid. Syria's descent into war-induced poverty has been dramatic. The World Bank described the economic impact between 2010 and 2017 thus:

> Estimates show that about 6 out of every 10 Syrians now live in extreme poverty because of the war. In the first 4 years after the onset of the conflict, approximately 538 thousand jobs were destroyed annually, with the result that 6.1 million Syrians are neither working, nor in any form of school or training. Unemployment among young people reached 78 percent in 2015... about 27 percent of all housing units have been destroyed or partially damaged across the cities covered in this study... cumulative losses in Gross Domestic Product over the course of the conflict have been estimated at $226 billion, about 4 times the Syrian GDP in 2010.[21]

A recent survey of young people by the ICRC paints a more personal picture of such pain and impoverishment. Talking with young Syrians in Syria, Lebanon and Germany revealed the following statistics:

- 47% had lost a relative or friend killed.
- 54% had lost contact with close relatives because of displacement and disappearance.
- 62% had been forced to leave their homes.
- 49% had seen such a reduction of income that they were now 'struggling for the basics', rising to 85% of young people still in Syria.

- 57% were missing years of education.
- 20% had delayed getting married and starting a family.[22]

Syria's warfare has also been comprehensively brutal, with consistent patterns of atrocities. Tens of thousands of men, boys and young women have been detained, tortured, starved, executed and disappeared. Thousands of the so-called 'Caesar' photographs of prison corpses smuggled out of Syria in 2014 show the extent of this torture and death in Syrian prisons. Millions of civilians have endured intense urban warfare, which has been a major cause of displacement. At one point, forty different urban areas controlled by rebel armed groups were deliberately encircled and held under siege by Syrian government forces. Throughout the war, government forces have bombed and besieged other civilian areas indiscriminately, joined by Russian air power from 2015 onwards. Chemical attacks have been frequent, killing and injuring thousands of people. Another particular signature atrocity of the Syrian war has been the constant bombing of hospitals and medical facilities. Physicians for Human Rights have evidence for some 600 attacks on medical facilities in the ten years of the war so far, the vast majority by Syrian or Russian forces. They estimate that an extraordinary 55% of medical personnel were killed in aerial bombing and artillery shelling during this time.[23] Throughout the war, aid convoys have been routinely searched for medical supplies, which were frequently confiscated, especially surgical equipment which might be used to treat wounded fighters and civilians. Medical staff were also regularly captured, detained and tortured for their part in caring for the enemy.

The ancient city of Aleppo was a widely publicized example of Syrian urban warfare. Aleppo had a population of 3.16 million people in 2010 before the war and was an early scene of protests for change in 2011. Armed conflict soon emerged across the city, which was cut in half from 2012 to 2016 between rebel-held eastern and northern Aleppo and government control of the rest of the city, with the famous Castillo Road as the frontline dividing the two zones. With Russia's entry into the war in 2015, the Syrian government's encirclement policy of 'kneel or starve' was changed to one of more intense offensives supported by Russian air power between June and December 2016.

The brutal 2016 air offensive is well described in a report by the Atlantic Council, a US think tank.[24] Some 4,045 barrel bombs were dropped on eastern Aleppo in 2016 alongside incendiary bombs and cluster munitions. Russian technology delivered these incendiary bombs in clusters of sub-munitions that resembled small napalm-like fire bombs. All these weapons are largely unguided munitions and fundamentally indiscriminate. There were reportedly also ten chemical attacks using chlorine barrel bombs. The government offensive was at its peak between September and December 2016 with 823 bombing incidents. In one month between 18 September and 19 October, Human Rights Watch calculated 950 different impact sites across eastern Aleppo, using satellite and witness data. There were 10 hospitals and 17 clinics operating in eastern Aleppo throughout the battle. These were routinely targeted and repeatedly hit from the air and in the land attacks by Syrian forces, Hizbullah and Iraqi Shia militias. Many civilians had fled previous barrel bombing in the years before the final battle, but the government line that there were 'only militants' remaining was not true. In early 2016, there were probably still 300,000 civilians in eastern Aleppo. The number continued to drop as more people opted for displacement, but most estimates still suggest there were 110,000 at the worst point of the offensive. Some 3,497 civilians were counted killed in the bombing of the final six months before 34,000 civilians were eventually evacuated in December 2016. The usual pattern of the summary execution or detention of men followed the taking of the enclave.

The localized war in northern Nigeria is an example of a type of sub-state marauding rural insurgency that is more common today than Syria's 'whole-country' war. Since 2009, government forces supported by local vigilante groups have been fighting against Boko Haram, an Islamist political movement and armed group which rejects rule by Nigeria's 'apostate' federal government, which it denounces for its godlessness and economic neglect of ordinary people. Between 2009 and early 2021, some 40,326 people have been reported violently killed in this conflict. About 50% of these were Boko Haram fighters, 45% were civilians and 5% were government forces.[25] Civilians have been killed by Boko Haram and by government forces and police, who have a long record of extra-judicial killing. A further 10,000 adults and children are estimated to have died from terrible conditions in government detention that has been widespread, brutal and without due process.[26] Boko Haram has also abducted and detained more than a thousand girls and boys between 2009 and 2018, partly in a tit-for-tat dynamic with government detentions.[27]

Professor Hilary Matfess describes how the tactic for a typical Boko Haram attack is 'to invade a village, slaughter the able-bodied men who refuse to join them, and abduct the women who have converted or seem amenable to conversion'. One of the girls she interviewed described her own abduction in more detail:

All the young men including Muslims were told to either join the insurgents or be killed. They slit the throats of some of the men, saying they'd not waste bullets on them. Christian women wearing trousers were shot in the leg and left to die. Older Muslim men and women wearing Muslim veils were released to go, while the rest of us were driven to their camp in the Sambisa forest.[28]

This murderous pattern of attack, with its signature atrocities, happened routinely in multiple violent incidents, which are sporadic and terrifying over long periods even if the death rate is more like Latin American gang violence than conventional warfare last century. Between 2011 and 2013, civilian deaths per month in such attacks exceeded 200 killings on three occasions. This was followed by a major surge in fighting during the military peak of the war so far between 2014 and 2015 in which monthly deaths peaked at more than 800 on three occasions before falling again. Monthly civilian deaths have exceeded 100 in only five of the months between 2016 and early 2021.[29]

This violence has still created a widespread social disaster. The UN estimates that 7 million people are at risk of hunger in the region because of the combination of violence and climate change. Movement restrictions due to military emergency laws have restricted farming, and climatic conditions are reducing yields. Fear of attack and restricted movement in the countryside has made rural life unliveable for millions of people, most of whom were already very poor. As a result, there has been a rush of rapid and unplanned urbanization in Maiduguri and other towns as people have fled from the countryside over the years. The demography and economy of the northern region has been totally transformed in ten years as the combination of war and climate change has made farming increasingly difficult and driven mass urbanization. The rural poor have become poorer and many of them have opted to become urban poor instead. In Maiduguri they are deprived of their assets and are unable to use their knowledge and skills as farmers, but they feel safer and closer to basic services.

The Nigerian war's violence against civilians—which is terrorizing, close-up and intimate killing in attacks on villages and towns by bullet, blade, bombs and suicide bombs—has forced 3.2 million people to flee across the four countries affected by the insurgency.[30] This illustrates, once again, the death–displacement ratio in twenty-first-century wars, which in this case is about 1:150 in 2020. Deepening poverty and war-induced hunger must also be taking lives and reducing life chances in an even wider population who remain in a climate fragile countryside under military restrictions on their movement and farming activity.

The wars in Syria and Nigeria reveal the common reality of war today. Attacks on civilian areas—whether by artillery and aerial bombardment or light weapons, knives and village burning—disperse, destitute and impoverish the civilian population. Intense socio-economic disruption is the deep crisis of war today much more than massive numbers of violent civilian deaths. The sheer terrorizing effect of attacks by governments and armed groups, and the frequent 'destruction of essentials', like social networks, businesses, jobs, farming, healthcare, education and cultural property, make life unliveable in certain areas. This forces people to move in large numbers, often becoming homeless, impoverished, sick and uneducated in the process. The social disaster of war can be counted in tens of millions of people and billions of dollars of development reversal, even if the number of violent deaths is counted in hundreds and thousands. On top of all this is the destruction of irreplaceable cultural heritage. Buildings, ancient spaces and artefacts, which are deeply sacred and precious to individual families and whole peoples, are carelessly or deliberately destroyed in acts of war and hatred. People lose family treasures, mosques, temples, churches, market places, libraries and museums to violence, and they are routinely forced to sell their family jewellery to pay for food, lodging, schooling and travel.

A Disaster on Top of Other Disasters

War may be only one of several disasters that a civilian population is enduring in twenty-first-century wars. People in or near war often experience a 'layering' of crises in their daily lives. War may be the most pressing social disaster but civilians may simultaneously be struggling with other high-risk conditions, like climate hazards, environmental degradation, migration, misogyny, failing governance and infectious diseases. Across the Sahel, for example, climate change and its intensification of drought and flooding often makes the disaster of war a final straw for rural communities who are already living on the edge of a sufficient and predictable agricultural livelihood. When war is combined with uncertainty about crop yields because of climate change, or the fact that a key family member has already migrated before the war, these compounding crises may prove too much for a family.[31] This compounded suffering is set to increase in the climate emergency. Already, more people are displaced by climate hazards than conflict, and many civilians in future wars will probably be recent climate migrants who have just fled from one disaster and are now living through another.[32]

The burden of risk from interlocking megatrends in people's lives often becomes too heavy and tips them into a final decision to migrate to towns and cities, relocate to a better rural area, disperse their family, or seek humanitarian help. It seems highly likely that many people who have moved to Maiduguri will not return to rural life if war ends, or they may only do so in part as circular seasonal migrants of some kind. Instead, many people may prefer to remain urban. In a growing city they may be less exposed to immediate climate risk and violence, while being closer to health, education and humanitarian services and, perhaps, a more liberal society where they may evade the full force of political megatrends like resurgent patriarchy and violent authoritarianism. Similarly, millions of Syrians will prefer the challenge of starting again as a migrant in Turkey, Jordan or Europe rather than returning to a greatly diminished Syria. Remembering the past and starting again in a new place may well be easier than returning and rebuilding for millions of Nigerians and Syrians because of war's effects, creeping environmental disaster and bad governance.

Gender and Civilian Experience

Dunant's account of war focused almost entirely on the fighting and wounding of male bodies. His thoughts of female suffering were confined to anxious women back home who were missing or mourning their men. He saw female strength only in this remote empathy and in the more immediate energy and care shown by volunteer women all around him who were 'ministering' to male bodies. Two centuries later, feminist researchers have revealed the full range of women's and men's wartime experience. They have described the important role that gender plays in shaping how wars are imagined and fought, how people experience its social impact and atrocities, and how they cope and survive. These social discoveries contribute essential insight to our understanding of civilian experience.

War has traditionally been conceived and practised within a patriarchal view, which sees strong active men fighting to protect vulnerable women and children. This stereotyped gendered script gives men lead roles and women important support roles as mothers, lovers, carers and peacemakers.[33] Men fight and women and children represent what they are fighting for—metaphorically as symbols of home and nation, or literally as prizes of war when men abduct and steal women and girls for rape and marriage, and boys for military service. Male and female bodies are also conventionally punished and humiliated differently in war. Men tend to be forcibly conscripted, detained, tortured and summarily executed more than women. Women suffer more sexual violence than men; their husbands may be ritually killed in front of them, and they may be ritually raped in front of their husbands. Many of these gender differences still hold in twenty-first-century wars but also vary because every conflict has its own gender norms and particular repertoire of violence and cruelty.

If Dunant focused his humanitarian concern on male suffering and courage, today's dominant view is that war affects women's lives worse than men's. It increases women's burden of responsibility and work, while the destruction of health and education systems reduces the life chances and life expectancy of women and girls more than men's.[34] Women and girls are understood to suffer most from displacement and sexual violence. It is estimated that women do more than men to keep their families together and feed and educate their children, and that they bear more psychological scars. It is, therefore, widely argued that gender inequality increases in war. Humanitarian agencies, and the Western governments who finance them, have promoted this view in the last twenty years. As a result, the suffering female civilian has achieved the same iconic status in the 2020s as Dunant's wounded male soldier in the 1860s.

This is a complete gender reversal in our image of the ultimate war victim. But is it right?

The discovery of the female civilian experience of war is a significant achievement and has greatly improved humanitarian aid and protection for women and girls this century. They are now more visible in humanitarian assessments, and aid programmes are explicitly targeted towards women and girls in protection, health, education, agriculture, cash-based income support and legal rights. Great efforts have also been made in law and practice to protect and support women through terrible cultures of wartime sexual violence. This violence is widespread in 75% of wars according to Professor Dana Cohen. Gang rape is especially common and is used to bond military men in armed groups and government forces in what Cohen scientifically describes as 'combatant socialization'—a form of group violence that increases social cohesion. Cohen also found that women were actively involved as perpetrators and observers in gang rapes.[35] Humanitarian action against sexual violence by armed forces has been further extended to reduce 'gender-based violence' (GBV) generally. This focuses on all kinds of violence against women, girls and LGBTQ+ people, including intimate partner violence (IPV), trafficking, harassment, emotional abuse and early marriage, as well as sexual violence. Importantly, women are now rising to senior positions across the humanitarian sector and bringing a more balanced gender perspective on civilian experience. This is helping to raise the profile of women's rights and needs and is increasing gender-sensitive programming in many agencies.

Feminist research is continuing to nuance our understanding of civilian gender and, moreover, to correct it in two important ways: first by ensuring that we do not overlook men and boys by misrepresenting the civilian as almost entirely female, and second by avoiding the tendency to stereotype women as victims. It is clear that women and men, girls and boys, experience the impact of war in different ways and in the same ways. They are all vulnerable to bombing and raiding, to forced displacement, impoverishment, ill health and hunger. But they also endure different pain, violence, burdens and responsibilities in war, like greater female risks of single-parenting responsibilities and sexual violence, and greater male risk of forced conscription, detention and summary execution. Such differences are significant and can be illustrated in two examples.

Risks in childbirth clearly affect women and new-born children disproportionately. A study in 2018 tracked the relationship between risks in childbirth and conflict-proximity across women in sub-Saharan Africa living within 50 kilometres of significant conflict.[36] This clearly showed that women living close to conflict are less likely to give birth safely in a health facility. There are sudden drops in deliveries in health facilities in the month that a violent incident takes place. Alarmingly, it then takes an average of three years for these facilities to reach birth levels that were normal before violence spiked. The study estimates that 47,000 extra births per year are happening outside health facilities because of conflict and this significantly increases mother and child mortality in childbirth.

In contrast, an Iraqi study of urban warfare offers a glimpse of male vulnerability. Its death and injury survey of Mosul some 29 months after the ferocious battle for the city looked at the experience of 1,200 households living under the Islamic State group (ISg) for 20 months and through the 9-month battle that ousted them. Under ISg, 0.71 men and 0.5 women were killed per thousand person-months. During the battle this rose significantly to 13.36 men and 8.33 women. Male deaths were consistently higher than women's and almost double during the battle because more men stayed to protect their property while women left in advance as IDPs, and because men were more likely to be targeted as a threat in the fight.[37]

Invisible Men and Pitiful Women

Despite distinct vulnerabilities and needs, men remain the forgotten civilians. Since 2005, Professor Charli Carpenter has consistently shown how politicians, militaries and humanitarians have been overly feminizing the civilian by repeatedly emphasizing 'women and children' as civilians and hardly mentioning men at all. She shows how this gender essentialism is disempowering women as stereotypical victims, rendering civilian men invisible, and distorting the principle of civilian immunity that legally applies regardless of gender.[38] In 2017, Chris Dolan of Makerere University noted how 'progress towards including men in humanitarian policy and legal discourse has been stunted, despite repeated attempts to challenge the silencing of men's experience'.[39]

This rhetorical and policy trend persists in 2021. The great majority of political statements and humanitarian programmes today lead with female concerns. Civilian men are implicitly stereotyped by humanitarians as relatively privileged, capable and resilient. Humanitarian discourse seems to imagine civilian men as detached from crisis and coping somewhere else with less significant needs because of the social advantages given by their gender. While humanitarians look away from men, political and military authorities in a war look directly at them as a threat and assume they are already, or could easily become, enemy combatants. This regularly puts men at great risk of death, detention and conscription. Yet, in the twenty-first century's militarily small wars, only a minority of men are in military forces in most conflict countries and are not a general threat. This leaves a majority who are civilians and also husbands, parents, carers, earners and survivors.

Carpenter's work shows how humanitarian agencies and Western governments have consciously chosen to emphasize 'women and children' strategically alongside other 'vulnerable groups' like the elderly and disabled in their humanitarian campaigning and programming this century. This is a powerful cross-cultural moral trope which, as a campaign strategy, may be more likely to concentrate political attention on war and suffering. The focus has also brought important new knowledge and expertise into humanitarian practice. But a 'women and children' frame is not a gendered approach to civilian experience and it misses out as much as it reveals when explaining civilian lives.

If the bias towards women and children's vulnerability is bad for men's civilian visibility, it also stereotypes women and children by promoting an old-fashioned image of them as weak victims of war who are in constant need of pity, help and protection. This is an absurd simplification. Many early twenty-first-century studies show how dynamic women are in conflict as earners, carers, rescuers, copers, adapters and organizers, and how the rapid social change brought about by war often opens up new space for women to act. Professor Marie Berry's study of women's power during and after the wars in Bosnia and Rwanda challenges the dominant humanitarian narratives of war, which mainly emphasize women's suffering, shame and victimhood. Instead, she shows how war creates major shifts in demography, economics and culture which can 'loosen the hold of traditional patriarchal and political power' and give women the opportunity to act. Berry's 260 interviews with

Rwandan and Bosnian women show how so many of them took up new roles in formal and informal political space to engage in 'everyday resistance' to war, poverty and suffering. They actively consoled and supported one another and their wider communities by forming widows' groups and credit groups, organizing aid, connecting with international agencies and achieving political office.[40] In short, women often achieve considerable wartime agency, some of which lasts into peacetime and transforms their societies in important ways, confirming for Berry the awkward paradox that war is destructive and socially creative at the same time.

One of the most famous examples of women's civilian action in war this century is the Women of Liberia Mass Action for Peace movement, which was formed by Christian and Muslim women's groups in 2002 during the Liberian Civil War. Led by Leymah Gbowee and Comfort Freeman (whose story is powerfully told in Gini Reticker's powerful 2008 film *Pray the Devil Back to Hell*[41]), this movement included women of all ages and classes, who used non-violent protests to campaign against the war and in support of women's rights. Dressed in white, their protest involved a permanent demonstration outside the presidential palace, a national sex strike, political lobbying, community radio broadcasts and intense deployment of maternal power to shame male politicians. In 2003, Leymah and a party of peace women stormed the peace process venue in Accra, where they mounted a sit-in and threatened to strip naked until the men agreed a peace.

Courageous movements like this one, frequently involving men and women, are common in war even though they are often violently suppressed. They can play an immediate role in changing the conflict and a lasting role in establishing new human rights norms in society. As Leymah said in her acceptance speech for the Nobel Peace Prize in 2011:

> Women had become the 'toy of war' for over-drugged young militias. Sexual abuse and exploitation spared no woman; we were raped and abused regardless of our age, religious or social status. A common scene daily was a mother watching her young son being forcibly recruited or her daughter being taken away as the wife of another drug-emboldened fighter… The world used to remember Liberia for child soldiers but they now remember our country for the white t-shirt women.[42]

Any view of civilians in war should be similarly balanced. Humanitarian policy should not simply see the many ways civilians suffer but also respect and support the many ways they act alone and together to survive and change the world around them.

4

Civilians as Survivors

The powerful role of women in surviving war shows how it is civilians—not humanitarians—who do most of the hard work of wartime survival. International humanitarian narratives, with their emphasis on victimhood and fundraising, still tend to lionize the agency of aid organizations and only partially allude to the agency of civilians themselves as the main actors in their protection, survival and recovery. In reality, aid agencies can only ever help some of the people, some of the time, and in a few ways. Most of the ingenuity, energy, labour and social capital that protects, feeds, finances, educates and heals civilians comes from civilians themselves acting as grandparents, mothers, fathers, siblings, children, workers, rescuers, engineers, medics, teachers, community leaders, activists and humanitarians. In various ways, these actions involve civilians resisting the inhumanity around them, often very bravely and with extraordinary stamina.

Civilians take exceptional actions and everyday actions to survive in war.[1] Exceptional action includes life-changing decisions to flee, fight or build something new. Fleeing is an extreme act. It involves actively walking away from your home, your work, your income and your assets, and leaving people and places that you love. It takes a major act of will and courage to flee because, although fleeing makes logical sense in the face of a serious threat, it is profoundly counter-intuitive at the same time. A decision to actively join the fight in some way is another exceptional act by civilians. It, too, involves a complete turnaround in somebody's life and a counter-intuitive decision to put their lives at risk rather than remove themselves from risk. Many young women and men make this choice, either to join armed forces of some kind or to commit themselves as political activists in the cause of war or peace.

Equally exceptional are people who suddenly turn their energy to build something new, like community groups to counter the human suffering of war by providing mutual aid, or creating social movements which struggle for peace. In every war today, civilians come together to build new organizations. Medics are starting, adapting, expanding and hiding clinics and hospitals. Teachers start new schools in bombed-out areas or under trees in IDP camps. Men, women and children start local aid groups, which often expand and link to international organizations for support. Many civilians join international humanitarian agencies and build huge aid programmes for their own communities. Farmers, science teachers, bank managers, engineers, jobless government officials and former soldiers suddenly become humanitarian workers in a dramatic new chapter of their lives. A great many children and young people work hard to build themselves by staying in school and learning, or by re-skilling in some way to adapt to new work opportunities.

Civilians' everyday actions are less extreme but equally essential for their survival.[2] Everyday civilian agency involves small but strategic acts that enable people's day-to-day existence and are endlessly repeated through a war. Much of this everyday effort is put into acts of kindness as families, neighbours and complete strangers help one another in small ways by sharing food, consolation, shelter, information and warnings. Much everyday agency is also taken up with avoidance, in a repertoire of daily actions by which civilians work around dangerous people and places to avoid risky encounters. Avoidance may mean taking a detour for a few extra miles to find water, go to school and get to work; or it may mean not answering the door and hiding when certain people come to call, and using deft tactics of absenteeism to make sure your name stays off a dangerous list. Civilian agency also goes into accommodating and negotiating the wartime power around one's family and community. Determined presenteeism in repeated queueing to be formally recognized by officialdom for distributions of various kinds requires civilians to wait for long periods and repeatedly tell their stories, fill in strange forms and answer curious questions. Negotiating a place in the system takes patience, time and tact. Sometimes it means being uncomfortably stereotyped, accommodating deliberate and unintentional insults, playing dumb or paying bribes and doing favours of various kinds.

Everyday civilian agency also rightly takes the form of active deceit and subversion when necessary. Civilians must sometimes pretend to be what they are not. They may need to give a good impression of political support to stay on the right side of a powerful party that they actually detest, or pretend to be someone's mother, brother or sister to rescue an endangered child, protect a vulnerable woman or smuggle a young man to safety. Civilians often find small ways to subvert and undermine the inhumanity around them. They may tell jokes, write graffiti or create artistic productions that question or ridicule the violent power around them. Civilians with an element of control over resources may tweak the policy of a government, armed group or international agency by breaking a rule every now and again to give a bit more here or there, or add excluded names to an unfair list.

International aid agencies, politicians and humanitarian lawyers have been slow to formally recognize civilian agency. They have tended to centre perpetrators, victims and their own organizations in their framing of war, aid and civilian experience. But this is changing, and civilian efforts to save themselves, resist inhumanity and secure their future is coming more clearly into view in humanitarian policy.

Recognizing civilian power means acknowledging people's capacity and decision-making, not just their vulnerability and their suffering. This extends to children, too, who are so often presented alongside women as the weak victims of war. In fact, they are often playing key roles in their family's present and future survival. Children may be working and caring for others to keep their family alive in the present, while also diligently learning at school in extremely difficult circumstances to ensure the family has an economic stake in a post-war future. Introducing their important 2004 research on children and youth on the frontline of war, Professors Jo Boyden and Joanna de Berry make this point about civilian strength:

> Even when confronted by appalling adversities, it is revealed that many people are able to influence their own fate and that of those who depend on them... The overwhelming lesson is that war does not inevitably destroy all that it touches, and that while war causes many to become extremely vulnerable, vulnerability does not itself preclude ability.[3]

Professor Erin Baines' work with women abducted by armed groups and their 'children born of war' has revealed the very active way that many civilians live as 'complex victims'.[4] These women were often treated terribly in armed groups and bravely struggled to resist in many small ways while they were with them, and they are now courageously trying to re-integrate back home. On one side, they are seen by their community as untrustworthy people forever contaminated by enemies. On the other hand, they are seen mainly as victims by aid workers. Neither side fully respects their pain and their courage. In reality, these women and their children are bravely resisting stigma and victimhood by daily struggling for their rights and a normal place in society.

Professor Claudia Seymour studied how young people cope and survive in DRC. She observed how the great majority of people are surviving by themselves without aid, and how young people often have to adopt 'high-risk coping strategies' like transactional sex, living on the streets and joining armed groups to survive the worst effects of the war and the routine everyday structural violence and poverty in which they live.[5] But many know exactly what they are doing and why they are doing it. Usually, they have chosen their life, not fallen into it. They have decided what offers their best way forward and acted accordingly. Aid was not an option for them.

Supporting Civilian Agency

Much has been learnt this century about wartime civilian agency. Research on disasters, refugees and resistance has usefully come together to shine a brighter light on how civilians survive and adapt in war. As a result, international humanitarians and their donating publics are slowly detoxing from endless images of starving children and white humanitarian heroes. Instead, aid agencies are moving to a view that de-centres their own significance and recognizes people's power and initiative in their own survival.

Modern disaster studies have always emphasized community-led action as fundamental to people's ability to prevent disaster and adapt to hazards like floods, earthquakes and hurricanes, and to guide high-level policy. Refugee research has similarly focused on supporting self-reliance and the maintenance of the public services and businesses that refugees need to survive and adapt. Humanitarians now try to avoid keeping people in camps and lining them up in long queues for food and water. The shift to cash-transfer programmes has helped to make this possible, too.

Studies of people's resistance to inhumanity and injustice in war have also emphasized civilian agency and have changed humanitarian practice. A resistance-based model of humanitarianism was the preferred approach to humanitarian action in the late twentieth-century wars and dictatorships in Latin America, often courageously pioneered by peasant associations, churches, trade unions and particular 'peace villages'. This tradition of non-violent civil resistance is crossing over to the more top-down colonial practice of wartime humanitarianism that has dominated in Africa. Civil resistance approaches, like protests, community-led dialogues with armed forces, community early warning and escape plans, international accompaniment, clandestine rescue, and mutual aid, have entered the humanitarian mainstream in the last ten years. The work of Peace Brigades International, Oxfam and important individual researchers, like Professors Oliver Kaplan, Erin Baines, Emily Paddon-Rhoades and many more, have helped to infuse resistance with more conservative Western humanitarianism as 'self-protection strategies', which, like disaster practice, focuses on civilian-led risk reduction and adaptation.

Civilian Attitudes and Influence

Civilians do not simply suffer, survive and resist war's violence: their wartime attitudes inform and shape the fight around them, actively contributing to war's politics and practice. And civilians are not all ardent peace activists. Civilian support for war is common, and they often approve of its violence against their enemies. Many studies show large numbers of civilian citizens in Western democracies offering strong support for their governments' foreign wars in countries like Afghanistan, Iraq and Syria. Many other Western citizens feel the opposite and actively campaign against the wars. The same is true in countries like Syria, Yemen, Iraq, Nigeria and Mali, where civilians take all sides and none in the conflicts that are destroying so much of their lives.

Poverty is often stereotyped as shaping pro-war civilian attitudes in the simplistic idea that being poor makes one more likely to adopt strategies of violence. This has created a popular mantra that poverty creates and sustains war. This is another policy myth. Typically, war's violence is not driven by poor people but by wealthy elite leaders who use military violence to repress popular demands, as in Syria, or by educated middle-class ideologues who take up arms to pursue a violent form of politics, such as Al Qaeda and Boko Haram, or by neo-conservatives who, for example, led the US invasion of Iraq. Once war is under way, poor people may decide to join one side or the other if military and support roles offer economic security and social status of some sort, or if political ideologues convince them of the truth and justice of their cause. Such poverty-based support of war is often driven by a person's sense of 'relative deprivation' rather than by absolute poverty—a sense that they are missing out while a minority is getting rich. Violence then offers opportunities to even things up. But war is mostly caused and driven by elites and is supported by a much wider cross-section of civilian society than is recognized by the poverty causation myth.

For example, civilian support for Islamist terrorism in the early twenty-first century was widespread, and it was somewhat surprising to find it in the type of person who agreed with violence that often deliberately targeted civilians like them. A study of fourteen Islamic countries in 2005 found that women were more likely to support terrorism than men, and that people with computers were more likely to support it than poorer people who lived offline. Generally, people who felt that Islam was under threat were the most likely to defend terrorist actions.[6] A 2010 study of civilian attitudes to Islamist militancy in Pakistan punctured four widespread myths about popular support for terrorism: there was no clear link between poverty and militancy; personal religiosity was not a major factor in support for militants; support for legal Islamist parties did not predict support for militancy; and democrats were not less supportive of violent militancy.[7] Western civilian support for UN-mandated wars against Islamist armed groups has been similarly wide and split, with all sections of the Western public embracing wars in Afghanistan, Iraq, Libya, Syria and Mali, while others in the same sections of society have objected to them.

The importance of civilian attitudes in legitimizing and enabling organized violence makes warring parties highly conscious of civilians as 'audiences' of war. All parties actively compete for civilian support on mainstream and social media in the information war that is such an important domain of warfare, giving and narrating their 'war performances' accordingly. In the Battle of Marawi, for example, both sides went to war with helmet cameras and phone cameras. The public information teams of the Islamist armed groups and the Filipino government forces then uploaded combat footage in almost real-time, with each giving it their own political spin in a second 'battle of narratives' around the conflict performed for civilian consumption.[8] The Islamists visualized and narrated a tale of heroic Jihadists bravely winning against a reckless and vengeful modern army with superior firepower. Government forces told of their careful and methodical advance, which spared their civilians and their troops in a vicious battle started by a murderous enemy who respects no rules.

Whether they support a war or not, civilians can also influence the way that war is fought, making it more or less violent depending on their attitude. Voting citizens can affect military policy as war goes along. Different civilian constituencies publicly and privately urge attack or restraint, or they argue for and against certain strategies and weapons in a fight. Civilian attitudes can incentivize incumbent politicians one way or the other by imposing political and electoral costs on decisions by wartime politicians.[9] The power of civilian influence holds true at the community level within a conflict, too, where government forces and armed groups may value civilian support and so adapt their methods of war to win civilian hearts and minds by protecting them and limiting violence.[10]

Influencing civilian attitudes by warring parties takes many forms. Information and misinformation campaigns on social media are one major source of influence, but many others are much more direct and interest based. In the Nigerian war, Boko Haram's marriage policy has changed attitudes towards the armed group and attracted young women and men to its ranks.[11] About 75% of the world's population live in societies that traditionally pay a bride price on marriage. As unemployment and poverty have steadily deepened across northern Nigeria in recent decades, bride prices have become impossibly high for millions of people and the prospect of marriage has often been deferred into people's late twenties and beyond, or it has been rendered effectively impossible with the person you love. Boko Haram wants young people to marry and build devoutly conservative Muslim families and so has subsidized and reformed the marriage market in areas under its control. It reduced the bride price significantly, paid it for couples from their violently procured profits, and set a rule that the wife should retain the money for herself alone. This rapid access to marriage at low cost and on relatively feminist terms influenced civilian attitudes to Boko Haram and caused many young people to join them.

But not all war policies are designed to accommodate civilian preferences. Civilians are also routinely punished with attacks and detention for having the wrong attitude: not giving their support, or giving their support to the wrong side, or to no side. This is obvious in the Syrian government bombing of rebel areas, and in Boko Haram's immediate murder of men who refuse to convert, and in the Nigerian government's widespread detention of suspected Boko Haram sympathizers.

Civilian attitudes towards the violence of war are sometimes, but not always, in line with the laws of war. ICRC studies show that a majority of civilians are in basic sympathy with humanitarian law's big moral rules, like the protection of civilians and prisoners, and legal limits on destruction in war, especially water and electrical supply, schools, hospitals and businesses.[12] Civilians in a conflict can even understand a justifiable moral and legal logic for why they are attacked and hurt. Professor Janina Dill asked eighty-seven Afghan civilians, whose families had experienced death and injury at the hands of the anti-Taliban Coalition's bombs, how they understood the morality of the attacks against them. Many families understood the terrible harm against them as unintended in a necessary effort to attack armed groups. They implicitly recognized two legal principles of distinction and military necessity, and many blamed armed groups as much as, or more than, Coalition forces for the fight that harmed them.[13]

But civilian buy-in to the laws of war is seldom unanimous or consistent over time. Sometimes civilians lose patience with the impartial, compartmentalized and highly reasoned legal logic of humanitarian law. Their legal buy-in is changed by events over the course of a war. If the ethical conduct of the fight deteriorates, many civilians soon adopt a different morality which breaks with principles in the laws of war in two main ways.

First, public commitments to military restraint and protection can snap if the other side breaks reciprocal legal agreements on the human treatment of prisoners of war or civilian immunity. Different studies of public attitudes in the USA by Professors Jonathan Chu, Scott Sagan and Benjamin Valentino show that American civilians may initially accept that US troops take greater risks with their own lives to protect foreign civilians. But if the enemy starts mistreating American prisoners or deliberately attacking US civilians, then a 'common sense morality' of tit-for-tat logic takes precedence and people lose moral patience with high standards in the laws of war.[14] Sagan's 2017 study showed that 60% of Americans would prioritize US military lives over foreign civilians, and it explains widespread US public support for nuclear weapons.[15]

Second, civilians are more likely to accept violations of the laws of war if they think their cause is existentially important. Professor Benjamin Valentino found that current levels of American respect for civilian protection is dependent on the extraordinarily low figure for US military deaths in recent wars. World War II saw US monthly losses peak at 9,200, compared to 485 in Vietnam and just 14 per month in Afghanistan since 2001.[16] In Valentino's experimental scenarios, in which a lot more Americans get hurt, public attitudes changed and US civilians felt justified in hurting a lot more enemy civilians. Many Americans, and several influential moral philosophers,[17] think that civilians who clearly and materially support an enemy should effectively lose their civilian protections because it is morally self-evident that civilians share liability in wars they actively support.

Valentino's experiments suggest that American acceptance of high enemy civilian casualties may well return if US death rates rise in future wars. We might expect a similar switch in public attitudes to war in other countries, too, even those which currently express strong preferences for civilian immunity. One side's civilians would no longer consider the lives of enemy civilians so precious if their own civilians were being aggressively targeted. Such civilian attitudes bode ill for big wars when the moral sense of warring societies may veer away from humanitarian norms. Sagan concludes that US public support for civilian immunity is 'shallow and easily overcome by the pressures of war.'[18] This probably holds true for other states, too. It suggests that maintaining humanitarian reciprocity in war is the most significant thing we can do to keep war relatively humane. Actual military conduct will determine the humanitarian character of big wars, not our innate compassion or our commitment to law.

The Digital Civilian

Millions of civilians live virtual as well as physical lives today in a way that Dunant could never have imagined. Digital connectivity has soared this century and created a large new area of civilian experience that is shaping people's ability to survive. Civilians are now present in both the virtual and physical spaces of a war. They have digital avatars on social media sites and exist as digital bodies in the medical, social and economic data banks that are fast-growing assets of governments, companies and humanitarian agencies.

In January 2021, the world population was 7.8 billion people. Some 5.22 billion people (66.6%) are unique mobile phone users. 4.66 billion (59.5%) are internet users and 4.2 billion (53.6%) are active users of social media. These figures are increasing year on year. The use of social media is rising especially fast, with 98.8% of users now accessing it via their phones. Indeed, mobiles are now firmly fixed as people's primary screen, with a global average of 4.10 hours per person per day spent on mobile devices.[19] Geographical network coverage for mobile and internet use now runs at 80% of the world's surface but, of course, not everybody has access or equal access to mobile phones and the internet. Many people use phones but less than 12% of people in less developed countries use the internet and, by 2023, around 3 billion people will not be using the internet if the current digital divide continues. Affordability remains a main barrier to connectivity. So, too, does gender. In many highly patriarchal cultures, like Pakistan, women and girls are often half as likely to own a phone. Censorship also plays a big part, with choices made by service providers and governments about who sees what.[20]

In many low-income countries with armed conflicts, connectivity may well be low and patterns of usage lean heavily to simple phone use. For example, in Yemen, 60.4% of people have a mobile phone but only 26.6% use the internet and 10.6% use social media. Across the Red Sea, in Ethiopia, 41% of people have mobile phones but only 19% use the internet and 5.5% use social media.[21] Connectivity cannot yet be assumed and many of the world's poorest people are still digitally excluded.

Even so, like so many of us, millions of civilians do have virtual 'data doubles' that live in the information space around war and humanitarian aid. This is especially true this century when wars are in middle-income countries in the Middle East, and in high-connectivity cultures like Somalia and Nigeria. Civilians show themselves on phone calls and social media, sometimes privately and intimately to their friends and family, and at other times publicly and politically as they actively participate in sharing images of war to the world in strategies of witness, protest and support. Civilian families rely on digital connectivity to keep in touch, share news, make plans and move money. This connectivity is vital to their survival and gives governments and humanitarian agencies a great way to connect them with life-saving information and aid.

Humanitarians are busy mapping, counting, coding, analysing, storing and sharing the digital bodies of millions of civilians worldwide. These activities are nothing new to humanitarian agencies, which have always counted, weighed and measured civilians, made lists of them with pen or typewriter, and kept notes from millions of interviews about their physical, social and economic lives. Historians, following Foucault, have long recognized such humanitarian processes in wartime as a pioneering force in international biopolitics. The numbers, lists and statistics of humanitarians have played a major role in consolidating fields of international government like nutrition, sanitation, development economics and global health. The COVID pandemic has proved the advantages of government having big data to inform health and economic policy, and of people being digitally connected to receive advice and aid, and to contribute their personal data on health tests and location to national crisis monitoring.

Last century, this was all done with index cards and filing cabinets, which created static paper avatars of millions of people. Today's much more revealing and mobile digital avatars, which can be instantly located, moved, analysed and communicated in real-time, offer great opportunities and risks for civilians. A digital life can keep people connected with each other and with government and humanitarian services. Civilians can receive digital payments in cash or voucher form, while their digital bodies can keep their place in important queues for food, vaccines and clean water. Digital data collection enables governments and humanitarians to store, compare and apply data on a huge new scale, and to use them more quickly to respond to changing circumstances.

But connectivity is dangerous, too, in an age of computerized warfare that is intensely digital. Alongside the benefits of a digital life as a civilian today, there are three main risks: military targeting; misinformation, disinformation and hate speech; and personal damage from a loss of privacy or from data inaccuracy. Civilians' virtual presence means that they can be under surveillance by warring parties, who may watch, track and target them in various ways. They may target them with helpful information—like warnings of attack or information about safe spaces and available services—or they may use their digital locations to physically attack or arrest them. Military intelligence agencies, journalists and human rights organizations alike all use AI to sift civilians' data presence—the photos, videos, text and locations they share— as open-source intelligence to understand a battle space remotely, identify key individuals, or piece together reports of human rights violations.[22]

Virtual space, especially social media, is also a battlefield in itself, where rumour, deceit and verbal violence create enmity, undermine the truth, and attack groups and individuals through strategies of misinformation, disinformation and hate speech (MDH).[23] Civilians on various sides of a conflict will often be actively engaging in MDH. They will also be its most likely victims when it terrorizes communities and becomes one of the reasons people decide to hide and flee, or when armed groups and angry mobs follow online instructions to attack them.

Careless data-handling or deliberate hacking can leave civilians exposed to physical identification and harassment, identity fraud, detention, or attack by warring parties and criminals. This places new high-tech pressures on humanitarians to ensure the data protection of people whose details they are collecting. [24] For example, in 2021, a database of biometric and family details of 830,000 Rohingya refugees in Bangladesh was controversially shared by UNHCR with the government of Myanmar—the same government that has been persecuting them for decades and whose military forces violently forcibly displaced them in 2017, killing and raping thousands of people in the process.[25]

We must expect civilians to be recognized and helped much more as digital bodies in the twenty-first century. As digital civilians, they have a new area of digital agency and responsibility in which to protect themselves and their families. Existing in two places at once, civilians will need to handle a twofold opportunity and risk accordingly by managing their digital identities and securing the protection and aid they need. Much civilian agency will be played out in computerized warfare, in which civilians will need to flee, hide, survive and build anew in virtual as well as physical space.

Part Three

HUMANITARIANS

At Solferino, Dunant imagined a humanitarian system for the world that would be a good balance of national and international response. Today's humanitarians, and the system they have built this century, are, therefore, my third main focus in this book. The Red Cross and Red Crescent Movement and the UN-led humanitarian system have made extraordinary progress in the last 160 years but have often emerged as a largely elite Western international system and not a broad-based global one. An intense elaboration of humanitarian ambition has also taken hold within the Western system, which goes way beyond simply saving lives. Humanitarians today are trying to address every wartime human need and building large intricate bureaucracies to do so. Aid work is becoming quite Baroque, its policies and practices embellished with hundreds of ornate social, economic and environmental objectives that aim to address every area of human life and human rights.

But is this system the right balance between national and international agencies envisaged by Dunant in 1859? I think not. Aid needs to change in the next ten years by responding effectively to two big questions that rightly haunt humanitarians today:

- Are international humanitarians overseeing a politically unacceptable and imperial system of humanitarian aid that operates a two-tier system of colonial elites and subject peoples?
- How should new-generation humanitarians ready themselves for the world's climate crisis and the possible return of big war?

5

Humanitarian Progress

There are about 570,000 humanitarians officially employed in the largest agencies of the formal international humanitarian system around the world today.[1] This number includes people employed in UN agencies, in international NGOs, and in the staff of the ICRC and other Red Cross and Red Crescent organizations operating globally. This is the international system that British humanitarian policymaker Ben Ramalingam calls 'Big Aid'. It does not count the many millions more people who work or volunteer at community level in religious organizations, Red Cross and Red Crescent national societies, community-based organizations (CBOs) and mutual aid initiatives of their own who self-organize beyond the official Western system. Nor does it count the hundreds of thousands of people who work in global networks of informal Muslim philanthropy or in diaspora-led aid in wars today, or South–South aid organized by China, India and other states who share resources and expertise with one another in systems beyond UN schemes. Even so, the official number marks a huge expansion in the formal international system of humanitarian aid in the twenty-first century so far.

Early in 2021, the UN's most senior humanitarian official identified 160 million people in urgent need across fifty-six countries, mostly because of conflict, and set out to reach them with some form of aid. He asked governments for $35 billion to do so and increased that figure to $39 billion with an extra appeal for COVID-related needs.[2] The UN-led international humanitarian system, its associated international NGOs, and Dunant's Red Cross and Red Crescent Movement have been built up by citizen activists and Western governments over the last hundred years. Today this international humanitarian network functions as a nascent global welfare system in many parts of the world by distributing food, healthcare, education, cash, and refugee protection to millions of people who might otherwise die or become even poorer and more destitute because of the wars around them.

In contrast to Dunant's minimalist vision of cleanliness, healthcare, food, water and letters home, many humanitarians in 2021 have their sights firmly set on a high form of welfarism where every human need is discovered and met, and where relief, development and peace join together in a single purpose. This ambitious project has grown slowly but surely with Western liberalism in the 160 years or so since Dunant worked for a few days as an international humanitarian volunteer.

An Entangled History

Dunant's description of himself in *A Memory of Solferino* helped to invent a new ideal of the humanitarian for the modern Western world. Dropping everything for others, like Jesus' famous Good Samaritan who crossed the road to help an injured man, Dunant rolled up his sleeves and got to work to repair the chaotic world around him and to restore its sense of humanity. He commanded, organized, supplied and cared. Although Dunant was only at Castiglione for a few days, and had never visited before, his memoir gives off an impression of his indispensability and his superiority to the disorganized villagers around him. Dunant the humanitarian was white, male, educated and enlightened and knew what was best. He recognized that the hundreds of people around him caring for the wounded, sick and dying were full of humanity—and ability, too. Their instincts were right and, if shown the way, they could be the main force in a worldwide humanitarian revolution.

This superior white male gaze and its paternalist tendency has run deeply through the 160-year history of wartime humanitarianism catalysed by Dunant.[3] It still does. But humanitarianism has equally always encompassed radical branches. Dunant's conservative state-centric Red Cross approach has always existed alongside a more radical and liberationist humanitarian tradition that challenges state power, especially in independence movements, socialist revolutions, wartime resistance movements, anti-racist struggles and the more solidarist Western NGO movements inspired by them.

Dunant cuts a heroic and original figure in his account of Solferino and in the way it has been presented and passed down by mainstream humanitarians. But the widespread idea that he is the sole founder of modern humanitarianism is not right. As Professor Johannes Paulmann and other humanitarian historians have shown, modern Western humanitarianism has an 'entangled history' and is marked in its evolution by many inventive individuals and several critical turning points.[4] Dunant is one of many founders of the modern humanitarian system, many of whom have been women. Indeed, Dunant's great hero was Florence Nightingale, who achieved humanitarian fame for improving hospitals for sick and wounded British soldiers in the Crimean War in the decade before Solferino. Dunant saw himself walking mostly in her footsteps. In the USA, Clara Barton, the founder of the American Red Cross, learnt nursing on the frontlines of the American Civil War and had much deeper operational experience than Dunant.

Women like Nightingale and Barton had an equally firm white gaze through which they saw the world and sought to improve it. Sadly and unsurprisingly, black women role models in the Western tradition—like Mary Seacole,

Sojourner Truth and Harriet Tubman—who also championed wartime nursing and war relief at the same time, seem to have been unknown to Dunant. Similarly overlooked by Dunant and the white Western humanitarian tradition is the great Algerian military leader Emir Abd al-Qadir, who fought a jihad against the invading French in the 1830s and 1840s in strict accordance with humanitarian rules and who went on to play a life-saving humanitarian mediation role in Syria's many religious pogroms. If the humanitarian moral instinct is universal, then it has obviously been made manifest throughout history by myriad other great individuals and exemplars across the colonized world, Latin America and China in the last two centuries. Humanitarian historians are gradually uncovering a more truthful history. But, even today, the predominant Western understanding of the modern foundations of wartime humanitarianism, and my own, are informed by whiteness.

This modern white Western humanitarianism has no single root. Most twenty-first-century humanitarians work in fields well beyond the provision of emergency healthcare that preoccupied Dunant, and so have many different ancestors. Humanitarians who work with the sick and wounded and deploy millions of volunteers in today's Red Cross and Red Crescent Movement, or in Médecins Sans Frontières, are the direct descendants of Dunant. But most humanitarians today spring from different genealogical branches. They are the direct descendants of the great humanitarians of World War I, some fifty-five years after Solferino, and of later humanitarian pioneers, resistance organizations, human rights organizations and anti-poverty activists in the second half of the twentieth century.

Humanitarians working with refugees or repatriating prisoners stand in the humanitarian tradition of the great Norwegian Fridtjof Nansen, who oversaw the repatriation of more than 400,000 prisoners of war after World War I and then became the League of Nations' first High Commissioner for Refugees. Humanitarians working in today's huge specialisms of food aid, economic livelihood and peacebuilding are descended from Quaker relief organizations. Above all, they are descended from one extraordinary American Quaker, Herbert Hoover, a mining magnate raised in poverty who turned humanitarian in World War I and subsequently became president of the United States. Hoover is the greatest Western humanitarian of all time and certainly had the greatest operational impact of any individual. He pioneered civilian rights, international food aid and urgent humanitarian diplomacy in Europe during and after World War I and in the famine of the Russian Civil War. Hoover designed and delivered industrial-scale relief operations for the industrial age, which helped save hundreds of millions of lives.[5] These operations may still stand as the fastest and largest of all time and are the precedents for today's biggest humanitarian organization, the UN's World Food Programme (WFP).

Humanitarians working on hunger and food security today are equally the intellectual descendants of the Nobel laureate Amartya Sen, whose 1970s research on the 1943 Bengal famine transformed humanitarian understanding of hunger and famine. Sen discovered that it is a lack of access and entitlement to food, and not a lack of food itself, that kills. This changed humanitarian policy. Many thousands of humanitarians who, like WFP, use cash-based relief programmes do so because of Muhammad Yunus, the great Bangladeshi founder of Grameen Bank, who pioneered and publicized pro-poor micro finance, proving its value to profoundly marginalized people, especially women, in the 1980s. Humanitarians trying to link cash transfers into wider government systems of social protection during the COVID crisis are inspired by former Brazilian President Lula da Silva's pro-poor Bolsa Família programme in the early 2000s and the Mexican government's earlier 1990s Oportunidades scheme. Many health agencies urging universal health coverage (UHC) are heirs of the great Welsh socialist Aneurin Bevan, who set up the National Health Service in Britain in 1945.

Humanitarians who work with children are direct descendants of Eglantyne Jebb and the group of liberal and socialist radicals who founded Save the Children in 1919 and who went on to promote a universal idea of childhood and the rights of the child. Jebb's successful identification of the child as a quintessentially innocent victim of war at the end of World War I parallels Dunant's successful recognition of the wounded soldier in the century before, and she looked to Dunant and the Red Cross as an internationalist model for her own organization.[6] Jebb's approach to the protection and development of children and childhood was taken up by the League of Nations and then by UNICEF and many subsequent child-focused NGOs.

Humanitarians working to protect civilians from violence and atrocity are descended from the anti-slavery movement and other humanitarian activists against colonial atrocities. Pierre Brazza, Emily Hobhouse, Roger Casement and Edmund Morel all worked to document and end colonial atrocities in Africa before World War I. They invented international human rights field reporting, public advocacy and parliamentary lobbying that are fundamental to modern humanitarian activism. Today's 'protection' work is also descended from the desperate efforts of the local Armenian humanitarian resistance network and the American Committee for Armenian and Syrian Relief (later the Near East Foundation) that struggled to keep Armenians safe and alive during and after the Ottoman genocide against them in World War I. Their grounded network of Armenian church leaders, businesspeople and volunteers, combined with US and European diplomats and missionaries, pioneered important aspects of humanitarian resistance and global humanitarian diplomacy that remain central today.[7] The International Rescue Committee (IRC), founded by Albert Einstein and others in the 1930s, and hundreds of resistance groups in World War II and in the Cold War conflicts and dictatorships, were similar protection pioneers who worked clandestinely to hide, rescue and care for people in danger in war and repression.

The advent of modern human rights after 1945 and the example of civil resistance movements led by Mahatma Gandhi, Rosa Parks, Martin Luther King, Nelson Mandela, Steve Biko, Desmond Tutu and hundreds more since then have greatly informed and influenced modern humanitarian protest, protection and campaigning. The Band Aid campaign, led by Bob Geldof to mobilize the world to stop the Ethiopian famine in 1985, was a peak moment in humanitarian protest and civil mobilization. The successful global campaign to ban landmines in the 1990s was another high point of late twentieth-century humanitarian activism.

Humanitarians today who object to the dominance of international humanitarian agencies and argue for more empowered, locally led humanitarian organizations and greater people's participation in humanitarian programming stand in a liberationist tradition of solidarity and self-reliance which many international NGOs and activist religious organizations pursued between the 1960s and early 1990s. These humanitarians work in a Marxist tradition of community consciousness-raising and political struggle, pioneered by Paulo Freire and Catholic liberation theologians in Latin America and the anti-apartheid movement in South

Africa. This humanitarian tradition often rejects neutrality and independence and signs up with one side of a conflict, as many did in the anti-apartheid movement and in the 1980s secessionist struggles in South Sudan, Eritrea and Tigray, and as did many liberationist movements against dictatorships in Latin America. Humanitarian support rooted in this tradition of political consciousness, self-reliance and social justice typically involves highly organized covert networks working courageously within their own societies and supported from afar by international agencies.

In contrast to this leftist liberationist tradition, Dunant stands at the source of the socially conservative Red Cross and Red Crescent model of humanitarian aid, which recognizes all governments, armed groups and political causes in equal measure, and whose national societies are usually firmly embedded in the governing establishment of a state. It is this politically agnostic Red Cross/Red Crescent model, with its first four fundamental principles of humanity, impartiality, neutrality and independence, that has set the tone for internationally recognized humanitarian action in the last thirty years. This 'Swiss model' of humanitarian aid has been taken up by states, the UN and international NGOs as the orthodox form of humanitarian aid during the neoliberal age from the 1990s onwards. It remains to be seen how China, Russia and Islamist middle powers now challenging Western liberalism decide to frame humanitarian aid in the next period of global history, and how new social movements of resistance to authoritarianism invent a humanitarianism of their own.

The laws of war, which humanitarian myth tends to present as founded solely by Dunant, have a similarly entangled history.[8] The first complete codification of the rules of war in modern times was American. General Order Number 100 was produced in 1863 at the request of Abraham Lincoln for Union Forces in the Civil War. Better known as the Lieber Code, after its Prussian-American author, Franz Lieber, it had 157 articles and was the first comprehensive attempt in the era of industrial warfare to strike an ethical balance between the military necessity of winning and a reasonable attempt to fight humanely in the process.

Lieber's ethical and legal balancing act has set the tone for all subsequent international treaties. A year after General Order 100, in 1864, the small conference of states inspired by Dunant's epiphany at Solferino produced the first international law of war in modern times. The First Geneva Convention and its ten articles specifically focused on protecting the wounded in war. Then, under Russian leadership from Tsar Nicholas II and his Estonian advisor Fyodor Martens, states and international law began to focus on the conduct of hostilities and on morally appropriate weapons in the Hague Peace Conferences of 1899 and 1907. These large gatherings had considerable civil society engagement, especially from the international women's peace movement, and the Hague Conventions banned gas, underwater mines, bombing from balloons, and starvation. Although many later treaties were finalized in Geneva as Geneva Conventions, Professor Boyd van Djik's historical research shows how, among other individuals and states, Washington and Moscow are the political capitals that have given consistent intellectual and political impetus to the modern laws of war.[9]

After World War I, Dunant's successors at the ICRC led on the issue of protecting prisoners of war, a vital wartime practice which the Red Cross had pioneered during the war, and states agreed a 1929 Geneva Convention on prisoners. At the same time, states asked the ICRC to start working on laws to protect non-combatants, or civilians as they came to be known. ICRC draft treaties were rejected in the run-up to World War II. In 1949, too late for millions of people, states agreed four new Geneva Conventions on the wounded and sick on land and at sea, on prisoners of war and, finally, on civilians. The new United Nations then led on important laws about weapons control and disarmament, banning chemical and biological weapons, and hosting nuclear disarmament talks and agreements. In 1977, states agreed two Additional Protocols to the Geneva Conventions, which learned lessons from recent decolonization wars and focused on civilians, the conduct of hostilities, and the provision of humanitarian relief in international and civil wars.

At the end of the twentieth century, the treaty to ban landmines was agreed by states in Ottawa in 1997. In 1998, the statute for the new International Criminal Court to prosecute and try persons responsible for major breaches of the laws of war, genocide, crimes against humanity, and the crime of aggression was signed in Rome. These two treaties were the cherries on the cake of an unprecedented half-century spent building up the laws of war and they brought humanitarian fame to two more Western cities.

From the 1960s onwards, the ICRC and states have increasingly renamed the laws of war as 'International Humanitarian Law' (IHL) and replaced the word war with 'armed conflict', partly because states wanted to dilute the idea that there may be a war in their country. Regrettably, this legalese has cleansed a word from legal and diplomatic discourse that is instantly associated in people's imaginations with horror, awe, honour, death and destruction. It has replaced it with a morally neutral phrase whose diplomatic politesse implies that war is a technical problem in international affairs to be legally and militarily resolved, rather than humankind's most brutal pursuit and a terrifying tragedy.

Humanitarian Achievement

The last hundred years of intense humanitarian law-making and impressive institution-building of international aid agencies have seen mixed progress of failures and amazing improvements. Terrible failures have left tens of millions of people dead. This is especially true of the genocides of

Namibian, Armenian, Jewish, Russian, Cambodian, Bangladeshi, Guatemalan and Rwandan peoples, where neither political will, humanitarian law, military force nor humanitarian aid was sufficient to save them. Aerial bombing in World War II, especially Allied firebombing and nuclear attacks, also killed millions of civilians. Political and war-induced famines have killed many millions more people, first in Germany, Austria, Armenia and East Africa during and after World War I, and then in the Russian Civil War from 1917 to 1922. In World War II, famine ravaged Bengal, Greece, the Netherlands, Henan Province in China, and Indonesia, and killed an estimated 1.5 million Russian prisoners of war, starved by their Nazi captors. Since 1945, there have been further devastating famines in China, Biafra, Bangladesh, Ethiopia, Sudan, Mozambique, South Sudan and Somalia, in which millions of people died who need not have died.[10]

All these tragedies are primarily political failures by governments rather than humanitarian failures by humanitarians, who typically lack the power to save people when confronted by political forces determined to make people suffer. But, as these humanitarian disasters took place around the world, an increasingly capable system of international humanitarian response took shape.[11] Simultaneously, alongside catastrophe, a history of humanitarian success emerged as humanitarians organized international systems of food aid, public health, legal protections and humanitarian diplomacy. This gradual humanitarian success can be illustrated by comparing two similar wartime scenarios in Syria but a hundred years apart. The comparison is not precise because one involves genocide and the other does not, but it still shows how today's international humanitarian operations have evolved to extraordinary effect from very small beginnings. Even if humanitarian aid is by no means totally or consistently successful today, it is an exponential improvement.

Syria 1916 and 2016

Syria in 2016 was the terrible epitome of early twenty-first-century war. But Syria has known hundreds of wars in its long history as a cradle and cauldron of human civilization. A hundred years earlier, in 1916, Syria was also steeped in war, forced displacement, civilian death and desperate attempts at humanitarian aid. The Ottoman Empire was fighting to save itself from the British and French Empires. At the same time, its new ultra-nationalist Turkish leaders were determined to rid the empire's core territory of all non-Turkic peoples and they used the war as an opportunity to perpetrate a genocide against its Armenian minority. In both 1916 and 2016, Aleppo became the focal point of civilian suffering for a time, but the difference in humanitarian outcome for forcibly displaced people in Aleppo in 1916 and in Aleppo in 2016 is striking. Aleppo in 2016 shows a level of humanitarian norms and a professional humanitarian safety-net in place for millions of displaced civilians, which was virtually non-existent for Armenians in 1916.

In 1916, Aleppo was a major hub in the Ottoman operation to deport and eradicate the Armenian minority. After massacring male elites in Armenian towns and villages across Anatolia, Ottoman police and soldiers forcibly deported the remaining Armenian population down into the dry and undeveloped areas of Syria. People were killed by starvation, typhus and massacre en route but hundreds of thousands of destitute Armenians still made it to Aleppo, which the government organized as a site for transit camps before people's final death march towards Deir Ezzor and the deserted drylands around it.

In 1916, there was no formal international humanitarian system to object and respond to this catastrophe. Instead, an informal humanitarian network of Armenian church leaders and businesspeople struggled to run orphanages, hide people with host families, and act as couriers to distribute cash to deported people. Many were killed for doing so or died from the deportation's typhus epidemic in the process. The Armenian humanitarian resistance network was supported by an improvised international network led by US and German diplomats, Swiss missionaries and German businessmen, who typically worked secretly to donate money, visit sites of displacement and massacre, and send written reports around the world.[12] The international effort was led by the US Ambassador in Constantinople, Henry Morgenthau, who quickly understood what was happening to the Armenians and raised political attention and financial support in the USA. This led to the founding of the American Committee for Armenian and Syrian Relief. The committee raised $60,000 immediately, which was wired directly to Morgenthau to distribute through his informal network.

This embryonic humanitarian response was never going to be enough to save so many destitute Armenians from death, but it was a landmark step in internationally organized wartime humanitarianism beyond Europe by the USA. The committee eventually raised $70 million between 1915 and 1921, which is about $1 billion today, and was the first international US NGO to receive a congressional charter. It saved many people affected by the collapse of the Ottoman Empire, including a vital remnant of 150,000 Armenian orphans. But this relief effort was no match for the earlier phases of persecution, deportation and deliberate destruction of hundreds of thousands of Armenians, their villages and their way of life.

A hundred years later, in 2016, Syria was entering the endgame of its latest war. Syrian, Russian and Iranian governments united to end Western-backed attempts to democratize Syria and competing Jihadist efforts to install an Islamist state. They were determined to destroy all opposition forces and re-take rebel-held areas. Since the start of the Syrian war in 2011, the full force of the modern international humanitarian system had been deployed to save as many Syrian lives as possible. In 2016, the Syrian government assault on rebel-held parts of Aleppo was relentless and civilians fled their homes over many months.

As in 1916, so in 2016, hundreds of thousands of destitute families were forced to abandon their homes, with only what they could carry, and start walking. As they fled, some of their men were rounded up to be detained, tortured or murdered. But most people were not forced to walk towards a desolate landscape without aid and so be devastated by hunger, disease and armed men. Instead, like the other 6.5 million internally displaced people in Syria's war, most of Aleppo's displaced people have survived. They walked towards an international system of humanitarian aid that has significant support, and they have been able to rely on some level of humanitarian order, which has restrained the warring parties to a degree. Millions of people have been housed in large converted buildings, hosted by other families, or have fled abroad to find international asylum. They have received regular cash grants or food, basic medical care and education. They have lost almost everything and suffered terribly, but they are alive.

The same is true for people in Darfur and for the Rohingya people in Myanmar in the early twenty-first century. Their case is even closer to the Armenians from the century before them because they, too, have been the victims of genocidal policies of dispersal and eradication. In Darfur from 2003 onwards, the Janjaweed militia, sponsored by the Khartoum government, pursued Ottoman-style tactics of killing, dispersal and destitution in hundreds of Darfuri villages. They murdered, raped, burnt houses and poisoned wells to make the villages unliveable, and drove hundreds of thousands of people into the arid landscape towards Chad. But, in 2003 and ever since, an international system of humanitarian response has been in place to give significant protection to millions of people in Darfur and neighbouring Chad after these attacks. International agencies established IDP camps and refugee camps that acted as immediate safety-nets and prevented people from dying in even larger numbers. People's lives have been extremely hard, but they have survived. They have endured two decades of enforced and unplanned urbanization instead of mass death.

The long-persecuted Rohingya people of Rakhine State in Myanmar experienced a similar fate in 2017 when hundreds of thousands of Rohingya were forced to flee to Bangladesh after yet another organized pogrom of murders, rapes and village-burnings by the Myanmar military. In Bangladesh, the government and the international humanitarian system came to people's rescue by supporting the establishment of an enormous area of improvised camps with shelter, food supply and basic health and education services. Like the displaced Darfuris, the Rohingyas now live in extremely precarious conditions with little work and at constant risk from fire, floods and cyclones. But the majority of them are alive and continue to have families. A hundred years ago, the survival figures for both Darfuris and Rohingya would most probably have been reversed. A majority of people would have been killed by enforced destitution and only a minority would have survived, as was the case for the Armenians.

These comparisons, over a hundred years apart, tell an impressive story. Today's international system of humanitarian aid is an extraordinary ethical and operational achievement in international relations. It has created significant consensus around humanitarian norms and the value of human life, and it has organized a form of international collective action which saves lives time after time.

Humanitarian Elaboration in the 2000s

This track record might suggest that life-saving alone would be sufficient ambition for today's humanitarians, but twenty-first-century humanitarians are determined to do much more for civilians in war than simply save their lives. Like their professional cousins who manage Western welfare systems, 'big aid' humanitarians want to understand individual human needs in minute detail and respond to them accordingly. As the academic disciples of Michel Foucault frequently observe, today's humanitarians are using wartime emergencies to take humanitarian governance to a whole new level. Their goal is to 'save and transform lives' according to the latest UN instructions for humanitarian leaders.[13] Safety, food, water and medicines are no longer enough. Humanitarian aid today has much more elaborate ambitions to be an advanced form of social work that operates a sophisticated socio-economic welfare system for hundreds of millions of people with very different needs in dozens of different countries.

Twenty-first-century humanitarians are trying to design aid programmes that reach up and down Abraham Maslow's famous pyramid of human needs, whilst applying the latest insights of Western social theory in the process. They want to address people's physical, social, economic, psychological and spiritual needs in a range of activities that support a person's basic need for shelter and their higher needs for self-esteem and personal empowerment in equal measure. Humanitarians feel mandated to work with people at such depth and breadth of need because of today's international legal framework of human rights and IHL. These two bodies of law recognize a person's right to almost everything good, while protecting them from almost everything bad. But is this ambition practical, and is it humanitarian aid?

Twenty-first-century humanitarians have developed an exponentially broad agenda of action. In particular, today's humanitarians are expanding their profession with major elaborations in five key areas: human identity; human needs; digital space; humanitarian time; and global welfare. New innovations in these areas now form the operational worldview of most 'big aid' humanitarians and have set in motion a continuous elaboration of humanitarian ideology, objectives, assessment and activity. In the process, today's humanitarians have recognized a proliferation of new needs that would have been unimaginable to Dunant at Solferino, and which make humanitarian aid increasingly ambitious, complicated, expensive and utopian.

Elaborating Humanity

Liberal theories of human identity have proved a rich field of discovery for humanitarians, who have used modern social theory to expand their core commitment to humanity. As humanitarianism's primary goal, the principle of humanity defines the profession's purpose 'to protect life and health, and ensure respect for the human being'. It is these last two words, *human being*, that humanitarians have been busy fleshing out in a more complicated human ontology, or theory of being human.

Like the liberal societies around them, Western humanitarians have recognized socially different ways that people experience and perform being human, as women, men, girls, boys, trans people, infants, differently abled people and elderly people. A person's ethnicity, colour, class or culture, and their virtual presence or absence in digital space, have also been increasingly uncovered as social attributes that shape a person's identity, experience, agency, needs and life chances in war. These social attributes, with their myriad differences, dramatically expand the obligations of humanitarianism's first principle by recognizing that humanity takes many forms not just one simple form. This commitment to a *diverse humanity* is now central to humanitarian ideology and practice.

Much of today's humanitarian aid, guided by people who have studied at universities that centre gender studies and critical social theory, is urgently attempting to accommodate the many differences people experience in being human. The overarching idea of intersectionality, a social theory from Professor Kimberlé Crenshaw and others working on critical race theory in the USA, is increasingly used to spot and respond to human diversity. Intersectionality recognizes that whoever stands before us is, like us, intersected by a number of different socio-economic attributes that affect their lives. For example, a person may be a black, elderly woman from a highly educated class, or a young, unemployed, white man with a chronic disease and a strong religious commitment. What they are determines how they experience the world. A person's class, colour, gender, sexuality, religion and economic status may all affect the way they are affected by a war and the kind of help they need to survive it.

This elaboration of humanity is revolutionizing humanitarianism. It is making humanitarianism's most fundamental principle of humanity as much about the micro-identities of individual human beings as it is a meta-identity for all human beings. From the nineteenth century onwards, humanitarians have always recognized different categories of human beings and appealed for their particular needs, as enslaved, wounded, sick, children, prisoners, women and displaced. Today's humanitarians are even more granular. They are pursuing a sort of nano-humanity, which breaks into the different categories within a single human person—their gender, class, culture, colour, ability, sexuality and age. They then appeal and programme for people, as different combinations of these identities intersect in individuals to form particular needs, as, for example, a female Tigrayan farmer in Ethiopia's war who is displaced in a majority Amhara town. Her gender, ethnicity and rurality will each influence the way she is seen, the skill set she has to survive, and the aid she needs.

This more elaborate understanding of humanity as both a micro-identity and a universal identity forms the new ideal theory of humanitarian aid. The theory goes that if humanity itself is not a singular experience but a more kaleidoscopic and varied reality for each person, then so, too, should be the business of applying the principle of humanity in today's relief programmes. Diverse humanity requires today's aid workers to carefully weigh and understand social differences in their humanitarian assessments and programme design so as to ensure that people's real needs are truly seen, rather than a biased set of needs wrongly perceived from the elite positionality of humanitarian workers.

Much humanitarian work today is, therefore, preoccupied with addressing intricate needs shaped by gender, ethnicity, ability and exclusion in an effort to connect with a person's unique identity and social role, and their resulting tendency to advantage and disadvantage, vulnerability and capability. Today's needs assessment requires aid workers to socially deconstruct the society and individuals around them. Not surprisingly, this means that designing and delivering a food distribution or livelihood programme has become a very complicated task, very different to some of the 'truck and chuck' programmes of last century. Defining so many individualized needs, and targeting aid accordingly, is a more subtle, time-consuming and expensive process than it was for Dunant in his wards full of a more homogenous caseload of wounded white male European soldiers.

Widening Needs

Looking more deeply into humanity itself and people's experience of war has caused humanitarians to discover new fields of human need, which they feel bound to address. Five new fields particularly stand out in the twenty-first century so far:

- mental health
- education
- climate adaptation

- accountability
- protection

These new needs have been routinely consolidated into humanitarian aid by a four-step process of organizational recognition, technical standardization, bureaucratic specialization, and diffusion to national offices and operating partners. Some of this standard-setting takes place in updates to the Sphere Standards (the sector's most detailed common standards), or in IASC (Inter-Agency Standing Committee) standards, individual agency good practice guides, or the sector-wide Core Humanitarian Standard (CHS).

Mental and emotional pain has recently been unanimously recognized as a core part of people's experience of war, alongside the thirst, hunger, injury and displacement of their bodies. Mental health, a long-time niche field of humanitarianism, is now championed as a major field of humanitarian need that demands massive projects in its own right. Humanitarian agencies argue that investments in mental health should be equal to those in physical health and are pitching new budgets and proposals that chart 'rising needs' in mental health, which require new forms of psycho-social programming.

Education has also been discovered as a humanitarian priority because the development of children's minds determines their ability to realize their full potential as human beings, which directly shapes their later life chances and the kind of jobs they get as adults. People in long conflicts want their children to keep going to school. So, a new humanitarian need for education has been recognized. New budgets have been prepared and funded, and a technical field known as 'education in emergencies' has become an integral part of humanitarian aid.

Climate mitigation and adaptation is rapidly securing its place in today's humanitarian repertoire. As humanitarians gear up for the world's climate crisis, they have agreed a new seven-point *Climate and Environment Charter for Humanitarian Organizations*.[14] This anticipates that millions of people worst affected by climate crisis will live in conflict countries. Climate crisis will be worse in war because many people's ability to mitigate and adapt will be deeply compromised by war's suffering, displacement and impoverishment, and by the fact that people often live beyond state control in war. Nor will their government be well placed to help because war often shatters public services, and a country's political volatility deprives a government of international climate finance. This all means that wartime humanitarians now feel bound to learn from their cousins in disaster management and become experts in community climate mitigation and adaptation in extreme situations. In addition to this, their climate charter rightly commits them to 'green' their own large organizations in a drive for net zero. If these commitments are to be delivered, it means new proposals, new specialists and bigger budgets.

Accountability is a complicated field that has been elaborately developed in two dimensions. First, governments who pay for humanitarian aid have instituted significant levels of reporting requirements for humanitarian agencies in the last twenty years. Many of these are extremely detailed accounting procedures that track expenditure and performance. These systems keep legions of humanitarians at their desks staring at Excel spreadsheets and lists of project indicators. When they are not filling in forms to explain what they have done, they are writing proposals asking for new money in ways that will appeal to donors and play into their preferences. For many thousands of people, this backroom industry makes humanitarian life much less daring and dashing than agency publicity suggests.

The second dimension of humanitarian accountability arises from a view of humanity that looks beyond bodily needs to civil rights. The new discipline of 'accountability to affected people' (AAP) is born of the discovery that the people humanitarians are trying to help are not only needy bodies and 'beneficiaries' of aid but also rights-holding and duty-bearing citizens who are entitled to a say in how they are helped, and who have a duty to help others in their community. Humanitarians are rightly discovering a social contract in humanitarian work between aid agency and citizen, and so forming a new understanding of humanitarian citizenship. Suffering citizens need aid to be 'relevant', 'people-centred' and transparent. They rightly want humanitarian aid and agencies to be influenced by citizen concerns, and to involve citizen organizations. This slowly emerging sense of a humanitarian contract between givers and receivers recognizes people as rights-holders and duty-bearers in decisions that affect them. But here, too, the instinct of humanitarian agencies is to bureaucratize, to prepare proposals, expensive budgets and specialists, and then meet this need with elaborate guidance for accountability processes that actively involve people, capture their views and act on them.[15] This is another organizational commitment to be bureaucratically delivered as a new field of activity when, in fact, it would be simpler if, instead, agencies could 'structure your work to be accountable, not to do accountability'.[16]

Perhaps the biggest field to be claimed and expanded by humanitarians so far this century is people's need for protection. From the late 1990s onwards, as humanitarians secured deeper access to communities in the middle of ongoing wars in Bosnia, Liberia, Sierra Leone and Afghanistan, they have put great efforts into developing programmes to try and protect civilians and keep them safe from attack, sexual violence, forced displacement, unlawful detention, human trafficking, early marriage, social stigma and family separation. As a sub-field of both protection and mental health, reducing and responding to gender-based violence has become a major specialism that covers many of these abuses and domestic violence. Humanitarian protection also goes further than protecting people from harm: it also tries to protect people's positive rights to land, documentation, citizenship and public services.

Protection needs have risen fast up the humanitarian agenda, and agencies have invested billions in large departments of protection specialists. In the wars of this century, humanitarians have tried to reframe all humanitarian work as 'protection-led', with humanitarian assistance like food and health being simply one way of protecting people among many others. The ability of humanitarians to protect people from major attacks, forced displacement, sexual violence, arrest and detention is obviously very limited. Instead, their work tends to help people pick up the pieces after major incidents and personal atrocities. Most humanitarian protection teams apply elaborate forms of protection practice, which combine field methods from human rights monitoring, incident reporting and civil resistance techniques, which are all agreed in a set of fifty standards.[17] These follow traditional human rights organizations and ICRC by putting together very detailed retrospective reports of violations of human rights and IHL, and using them to engage in often fruitless 'protection dialogues' with warring parties to try to improve conditions for civilians. Protection practice also copies national human rights defenders and Peace Brigades International by deploying strategic presence and accompaniment by humanitarian staff to ensure safe spaces for civilian communities. They also draw on threatened communities' civil resistance experience to apply methods of community-based 'self-protection' by early warning of attacks, hiding, evacuation and routine negotiation and accommodation with warring parties.

As more and more humanitarians themselves have been killed, their own protection needs have become increasingly important; staff security has become a major new area of humanitarian aid, and yet another area that is being elaborately systematized and bureaucratized. This combines passive security measures, the cultivation of acceptance, and continuous frontline negotiation. This, too, increases humanitarian costs and agency staff. Finally, and ironically, people need protecting from humanitarians themselves, some of whom have been responsible for sexual violence, sexual exploitation, bullying and harassment in their aid programmes. This has given rise to a major new workstream to prevent sexual exploitation and abuse (PSEA), which requires yet more staff, procedures and money to ensure the safeguarding of people receiving aid and of employees inside humanitarian agencies.

Expanding in Digital Space and Digital Money

Digital technology has transformed humanitarian assessments, communications, aid delivery and project management. For example, the single biggest change in humanitarian aid in the last twenty years has been the direct distribution of cash to people suffering in war. In 2004, only 1% of humanitarian aid was delivered to people as cash, with most of it distributed in kind as food, shelter materials, clothing, medicines, seeds and tools. In 2019, this had risen to 18% of aid, with cash transfers totalling $5.7 billion that year. [18] The enormous increase in cash transfers has been greatly accelerated by digital transfers. Cash is quicker and logistically simpler if there are still functioning markets around civilians where they can buy food and other essentials. Much of this cash is transferred digitally through humanitarian debit cards and mobile phone transfers. Two giant international agencies, UNHCR and WFP, are responsible for 60% of these transfers. WFP's adoption of cash has rocketed from $10 million in 2009 to $2.1 billion in 2019. But suppliers are diversifying, and the Turkish Red Crescent and the Kenyan Red Cross are examples of two national organizations that are world leaders in humanitarian cash. Cash transfers are widely recognized as more dignifying for people because they respect people's personal agency. They can receive cash without queueing for hours and are free to make their own household choices about priorities and expenditure. Evidence also suggests that injections of cash grow people's local economy better than aid in kind.

Digitalization of humanitarian data and aid is the fastest-moving development in humanitarian work today. The use of satellites, mapping programmes, big data and huge volunteer teams of 'digital humanitarians' is transforming the way war and disaster are monitored and aid is targeted and distributed in real-time. Patrick Meier, a pioneer of the field, sees the change as empowering affected communities and big agencies alike:

> Disaster affected communities are increasingly becoming 'digital communities' as well… more and more people around the world turn to social media to communicate during disasters, but they also use these and other platforms to self-organize in response to crisis—often faster and more efficiently than traditional humanitarian organizations.[19]

Meier gives many examples of how information on digital platforms has saved lives and created important systems of mutual aid at the local, national and international level by sharing details of warnings, safe sites, food and medical services. Crowd-sourced mapping is now routinely helping agencies like UNHCR and MSF to understand the movement and settlement of displaced people. More forensically, it is being used to identify those involved in war crimes and other violations of IHL and human rights. In all these efforts, Meier rightly warns against 'false data', which are deliberately misleading, and 'data bias', which is prone to 'spotlight' communities that are digitally visible and ignore those that are offline. Both risks will have to be managed by digital humanitarians as they find the right way to balance digital and manual responses in the wars and crises ahead.

In 2014, the UN launched the Humanitarian Data Exchange (HDX) in The Hague. By early 2021, this had 18,962 different datasets sourced from 1,427 different sources and covering 254 locations. HDX reported that its platform had 289 organizations sharing their data and had 1.3 million users. HDX is working hard to curate and scale-up these various datasets into coherent 'data grids' for particular problems and places which can 'turn data into insights'.[20] Many humanitarians today are engaged full-time in gathering, processing and analysing digital data about population movements, health and food needs, protection needs and poverty. They also monitor and measure programme performance with digital data and engage digitally with people, sharing life-saving advice and information and moving personal messages between separated families. Humanitarians are using satellites, drones and algorithmic programmes of all kinds to gather data about human rights violations, war-related damage, drought, floods and living conditions. They are storing these data themselves and sharing them with others. Many aid agencies are now combining their local data into big data to anticipate crisis and ensure early response in a new method of 'forecast-based financing'. This uses data analysis to predict hunger, flooding, asset damage or displacement and proactively triggers aid funds to support people at risk before disaster strikes.[21] This important new emphasis on anticipation and anticipatory aid will play a major role in the escalating humanitarian response to increasing climate hazards and displacement in and out of war zones in the next ten years.

Leveraging greater humanitarian success from improved data will also rely heavily on the 'interoperability' of humanitarian data. Technically, this requires humanitarian agencies to agree the same data standards to be sure that all humanitarian data in general use are good quality, safe and professionally interpreted.[22] Politically, it means agencies being ready to share their data. Here, inter-agency competition is already coming into play because good data are a commercial advantage which makes an agency more likely to get government funding and a glowing reputation. Sadly, we can expect some agencies to become data hoarders or share their data late after they have exploited the data themselves. Rules on data-sharing must be an essential part of data regulation across the humanitarian sector.

In the next ten years, humanitarians will be working as much in the digital lives of civilians as in their physical lives. Aid agencies can expect an exponential increase in the volume of data they generate, hold, share and use. They can also expect to rely on more and more artificial intelligence applications to help them collect, sift and interpret humanitarian data, and then deliver aid. This is already creating big challenges of data security and data protection for agencies and for individual civilians whose data and digital lives they hold and share.[23]

Too little access to data will also become as much a problem as too much access. Just as humanitarians routinely have problems of physical access to people in need, so they can expect increasing access problems in digital space. Recent crises in Tigray and Myanmar show how governments will increasingly shut down and manipulate people's digital connectivity in conflict. People will frequently be forced offline as the internet is weaponized in various ways. Humanitarians will face checkpoints, obstruction, risks and attacks in digital space similar to the ones that restrict their access in physical space. Many people in need will be held beyond their digital reach.

Long Aid and the Extension of Humanitarian Time

Working in long wars where people are displaced and impoverished for decades, and now anticipating years of climate crisis ahead, has given humanitarians a new sense of time and a new commitment to long aid. The frequent withdrawal of development aid and finance from volatile conflict areas has made this challenge more pressing still. Even if the World Bank has recently recommitted to invest in wartime,[24] many governments and international finance institutions (IFIs) still consider it too risky, or they deliberately restrict investment under political sanctions and counter-terror legislation. This development vacuum in wartime brings new ethical challenges to humanitarians, who feel duty bound to lean into support for infrastructure

194

investment and development programming that would more usually be done by development agencies.

This longer time horizon and development gap-filling has complicated humanitarian aid and driven up its costs. No longer do humanitarians see themselves solely as urgent relief services helping people through a bad harvest or a temporary displacement, and then reverting to development work or leaving for the next disaster. Instead, their time horizon has changed, and with it the range of their moral responsibility. Today's humanitarians feel responsible for saving people's lives, improving their livelihoods, helping them adapt to climate change, restoring people's dignity and protecting all their human rights. As a result, humanitarians have set longer-term goals, and seen new business opportunities in accompanying communities in crisis over years to achieve a level of resilience, especially when development organizations flee from war, taking their aid money with them.

Most humanitarians today are not working in the immediate violence of war and destruction but rather with large groups of people enduring the consequences of war for many years in unplanned urban settlements of displaced people or badly damaged and deprived rural areas. Here, humanitarians try to build and maintain basic services like health, water and education for years in a seemingly endless process of long aid. Many twenty-first-century agencies are in their second or third decade of work with communities in Afghanistan, Myanmar, Iraq, Syria, South Sudan and

DRC. The most extreme example of such long aid to people affected by war is UNRWA's (United Nations Relief and Work Agency) ongoing work with Palestinian refugee communities from the 1948 Arab–Israeli War. Much wartime aid today is becoming similarly routine and entrenched for decades like UNRWA's long aid.

Humanitarians are almost unanimous in thinking their aid must have some lasting effect that helps people in a sustainable way not just this month but next year too. Professor Thea Hilhorst has described this trend as a shift from 'classical humanitarianism' to 'resilience humanitarianism', which sees humanitarians working to achieve long-term development objectives as well as life-saving ones.[25] This extension of humanitarian ambition through time is best shown by its changing discourse. Immediate humanitarian objectives to deliver food, medicines, cash, seeds and tools have deepened to support people's food security, health security, water security and livelihood security. Humanitarians want to give people a fishing rod and a well-stocked lake, not just a fish. Their intention is to have a 'sustainable humanitarian impact'[26]— which increases the resilience of basic services, markets and individuals—now a system-wide ambition in a so-called 'nexus' policy that combines humanitarian, development and peace activities towards 'collective outcomes' and 'durable solutions' and 'achievement of the sustainable development goals'.[27]

This extended sense of humanitarian time and the importance of sustainable impact sees humanitarians deliberately engaging more deeply in societies. They are investing in the repair, improvement and ongoing maintenance of large urban infrastructure to secure lasting water and electrical supply for urban populations, their schools and businesses. Humanitarians want to sustain functioning health systems rather than just clinics; functioning markets and food systems, not just food aid; and sustainable jobs and small business development, not just cash grants. They are working to improve gender relations and gender justice in societies and to reduce gender-based violence of all kinds, and they are working with disabled people to increase their access and inclusion in society. Much of this humanitarian work is often indistinguishable from community development work. But not all humanitarian workers know how to do development well, or have the scope to do it well. Many are learning on the job while under pressure from twelve-month budget cycles that may or may not be renewed, instead of well-researched multi-year planning and financing.

Globalizing Welfare

Many of these trends have recently come together in humanitarians' new fascination and engagement with national social protection schemes. An extended time horizon, a deeper and sustainable social mission and the scaling of cash transfers means humanitarian aid is now in a position, ideologically and technically, to join government and development colleagues in improving the flexibility of national social protection systems. In other words, humanitarians are now increasingly committed to supporting the expansion of the welfare state in many low-income countries around the world whose populations are at high risk from conflict, the consequences of COVID and increasing climate crisis.

Social protection programmes are the responsibility of government and refer to a range of individualized welfare schemes. These may be *contributory*, where people pay into a social insurance system for healthcare, pensions and unemployment benefit, or give their labour in public works like building roads or planting trees and building walls as climate mitigation measures. Or, they can involve *non-contributory* 'social assistance' schemes, in which people are simply given things in cash or kind with the specific purpose of protecting their livelihoods, health, shelter and education, or training them in new skills. Most government social protection has an ambition to provide 'full lifecycle' support from cradle to grave, which is now recognized by all states in the UN's Sustainable Development Goal 1.3.

Humanitarian interest in predictable, sustainable support to crisis-prone populations has grown steadily over the last forty years, surging dramatically this century in the Middle East wars and the global COVID crisis. Back in the 1980s, in

Ethiopia and other drought-prone countries of the Sahel, organizations like Save the Children, Oxfam, UN agencies and the World Bank worked with rural populations to set up programmes to predict hunger and prevent famine by creating 'safety-nets' of various kinds. These typically included early warning systems, food aid, school meals, water storage cisterns, grain and seed banks, public works programmes and public health investment. The most detailed and influential system was the Household Economy Approach (HEA) developed by Save the Children and the UN's Food and Agricultural Organisation (FAO) in the 1990s. It was the government of Ethiopia that then pioneered a comprehensive national system—the Productive Safety Net Programme (PNSP). By 2008, the PSNP was supporting 7–8 million people a year, 'catching' people with cash or in-kind support before they fell into hunger and asset-selling, and hoping that sustained support would enable people to 'graduate' out of poverty into a more self-reliant and resilient livelihood.[28]

Huge Syrian refugee populations this century in Turkey, Lebanon and Jordan created a big new surge of cash-based social protection programming by humanitarians who found themselves operating in middle-income countries whose governments already had relatively developed social protection systems in place. This level of welfare sophistication was a new experience for humanitarians more used to working in countries like Somalia, DRC and

South Sudan. Since 2011, agencies like UNHCR, WFP, UNICEF, IFRC (International Federation of Red Cross and Red Crescent Societies) and many INGOs have aligned with government policy in these three countries and designed cash-based systems for refugees and host families which now function as relatively elaborate forms of social protection for millions of people.

In 2020, the COVID crisis exponentially increased humanitarian engagement in national social protection efforts all around the world. Between March 2020 and May 2021, a total of 3,333 new social protection measures was being planned or implemented by governments in 222 countries around the world to counter the health, education and economic shocks of the COVID crisis—a rise of 148% since December 2020. Social assistance schemes soared by 120% and labour market interventions (mainly cash-based job protection schemes) surged by 330%. Most COVID response schemes have been social assistance and the vast majority of these have been in direct cash transfers, with 734 new cash assistance schemes in 186 countries.[29]

Humanitarians are joining this rush into social protection and are finding ways to add humanitarian aid into wider social protection programmes by 'linking' and 'surging' with national systems in 'shock-responsive' social protection. Recognizing that social protection is a government responsibility, humanitarians are adding value to national systems in two main ways. First, they are reaching out to people who are beyond a state's current social protection 'register' (its national list of vulnerable people) to bring millions of affected people into the programme, so increasing the *coverage* of government schemes. Second, humanitarians are also helping by topping-up government contributions to ensure the *adequacy* of social protection schemes when they are most stretched. For example, Kenya Red Cross is operational in all of Kenya's forty-seven counties. During the COVID crisis, it has helped top-up government payments in several counties and brought large numbers of new vulnerable people in its own cash programmes into the government's social protection system by including them in a single national register.[30]

The COVID crisis has ensured that social protection is now fixed as a major new field in humanitarian aid. Several Western governments are firmly backing humanitarian synergy with social protection as a core pillar of humanitarian response at a time when all conflict-affected and disaster-prone countries are developing their social protection systems fast. The British government's SPACE programme (social protection approaches to COVID-19) worked with governments and humanitarians to expand national social protection systems in forty-two low-income countries in 2020, with a strong focus on linking humanitarian aid to expanding government social protection schemes. Social protection is now growing faster than other humanitarian approaches because it offers a national one-stop shop for meeting a wide variety of people's needs and can leverage digital technology in its assessment, targeting and delivery. If humanitarians get cash and social protection systems right, they can address people's needs for healthcare, education, livelihood and shelter through a single digitalized system wherever there is a functioning market or sufficient institutions for people to access these public goods. Cash transfers also help to attract and build these markets and institutions.

Looking ahead, social protection is the big system people will need for the intense periods of climate crisis coming towards them in the next ten years. It will not always be the case that there is the opportunity to combine humanitarian aid with social protection systems, but it will often be the case. Linkage makes good sense when a government is developing social protection and wants to operate an impartial system that permits humanitarians to play their outrider role to expand participation in social protection and boost its inputs at critical moments of extreme shock. As a general rule, unless war is polarizing a whole society and government is deliberately marginalizing enemy people, it must always be better to coordinate and integrate international humanitarian efforts with national social protection instead of creating parallel systems run by internationals. These inevitably disempower and compete with government efforts. The exception is in rebel-controlled areas where government systems no longer reach and where alternative systems will need to be created.

A Needy Profession

In their constant elaboration of humanitarian aid, Western humanitarians claim to have uncovered a world of growing and increasingly complex needs in this new century, which are regularly detailed in the 'more than ever' shopping lists of UN, Red Cross and NGO leaders. We hear constantly that 'needs are rising' and that the 'gap between needs and response' is widening exponentially each year. And yet, today's wars are militarily small wars and large famines have been rare in the last twenty years. Death rates are low compared to previous centuries and humanitarian aid budgets have kept rising almost year on year. So why are humanitarians so needy? There are perhaps two reasons.

First, because some of the needs they want to meet stem from deeply structural problems or megatrends that pre-exist wartime suffering. Many immediate needs experienced by civilian populations arise from attack, displacement, destitution, hunger, sickness and educational disruption that are specifically war related. But many of the 'escalating', 'multiplying' and 'compounding' needs that humanitarians proclaim do not arise solely from people's wartime suffering: they were an entrenched part of life before the war, or they are the projections of Western humanitarians who see the needs of wartime societies around the world in their own liberal image. 'Big aid' humanitarian leaders have decided to embrace the struggle for gender equality and an end to GBV in places where gendered suffering was often a huge challenge before the war and long embedded in patriarchal norms and violence. They have also decided to support the ideal of a welfare state and free public services wherever they can, in places where political corruption, low tax bases, negligent governments and inadequate social contracts between state services and citizens made this deeply problematic long before the war. Megatrends like climate crisis, migration and entrenched poverty combine with war to create severe humanitarian needs, but they, too, precede war and will continue after war as deep problems for post-war societies.

In other words, humanitarians are engaging with pre-existent and potentially endless needs and, as a result, are endlessly working. Humanitarian ambition to meet these huge needs for deep structural change has extended the operational depth, time horizon and complexity of their work. They have deliberately chosen to complicate their mission and work with a long-term developmental ambition and with democratic commitments to create liberal societies. These choices mean that humanitarians are often politically engaged in changing society at a deeper level than its war-torn damage. Not surprisingly, their list of 'needs' is wide and long. In places like Afghanistan and Iraq, UN agencies and many NGOs have gone in deep under the wing of Western military forces and Western government budgets, or with similar UN mandates in DRC, CAR, Somalia and other conflicted countries across the Sahel. They have embraced development mandates as much as humanitarian ones.

In short, there is a lot going on in Western humanitarian aid alongside the promotional rhetoric of urgent life-saving and protection. As a Western liberal, I share a lot of these ambitions for others and for global society at large. But this is only one way to be humanitarian. There are also other ways that are grounded in different social traditions of conservative patriarchy, or in authoritarian, green, socialist or Islamist ideologies. A humanitarian working in these traditions can also 'protect life and health, and ensure respect for the human being' *in extremis*, as many do in Muslim networks worldwide and diaspora aid not counted by the UN system. But she or he may not want to struggle simultaneously for gender equality, LGBT rights, a capitalist market economy and a welfare state answerable to a free-thinking population. It is important, therefore, for Western humanitarians to recognize that compassion and its desire for life-saving may be universal, but that much of what they elaborate around it may not be, and may well be seen as interference rather than humanity.

The second reason that Western humanitarians are so needy is because their organizations are so costly. The way humanitarian organizations operate as global bureaucracies creates huge organizational needs in recurrent costs that are extremely expensive to maintain. This means that perhaps the biggest and most expensive humanitarian needs today are institutional. Billions of dollars are needed to pay for the international administration required to organize all these elaborate demands into programmed activities by large global bureaucracies. Technical diversification into education, mental health, social protection and climate adaptation, as well as a desire to protect every area of human rights, leads humanitarians into big new targets, new specialisms, new technical units, expanding bureaucracy and constant budgetary growth inside their organizations. 'Big aid' leaders have not yet adapted their business model to break up their bureaucracies, improve their value for money, and maximize their impact in these different fields. Instead, they focus on the need to expand and control every elaboration in a single bureaucracy, so overheads are huge. As a result, the 'big aid' agencies need more and more money every December to keep going and growing for another year. They are set on a path of building bigger and bigger operational superagencies to deal with everything, and hope that their Western government donors view them as too big to fail. The exceptions are the national societies of the Red Cross and Red Crescent Movement and the independent national affiliates of the churches and some international NGOs. These are more decentralized, devolved and autonomous organizations that are much more in line with Dunant's vision. They are cheaper to run and better placed to spread costs more evenly and create genuinely broad-based and citizen-led humanitarian institutions at the national and sub-national levels.

The 'big aid' model of growth centres too much on international organizational needs and not the needs of suffering civilians. For example, the 'need' for expensive global AAP or protection teams costing many millions of dollars per year is an organizational need but not necessarily a need that would be expressed by people experiencing violent attacks or gender-based violence, or communities wanting more power over the distribution of aid. They are the institutional needs of humanitarians and may not always align with how people would spend the equivalent money if it were put directly into their hands. Endangered civilians might find better and cheaper ways of improving their immediate situation and their campaigns for lasting social change. Or they might opt to pay their way out of a crisis but leave society largely unchanged.

Recovering Humanitarian Purpose

The elaboration of humanitarian need, ambition and capacity in the last twenty years has confused the overall purpose of humanitarian aid. Its 'do everything' approach has left humanitarian effectiveness hard to gauge when success is dispersed across so many different sectors and ambitions. In 2016, Professor Shandiz Moslehi and her team made a meta-review of hundreds of recent humanitarian evaluations to understand their common definition of humanitarian success. It was a doomed task. Instead of a clear and common purpose she found forty-eight recurring characteristics of effectiveness. These included food security, women's empowerment, risk reduction, increased resilience, securing children's futures, respecting humanitarian principles, building local capacity, value for money, involving the private sector, community engagement, transparency and many more. She rightly concluded that the humanitarian system's overall humanitarian objectives are 'vague' with no standard definition of effectiveness in humanitarian aid today. Importantly, Moslehi also found that humanitarian evaluations are heavily biased towards reporting what went well not badly, and that the forty-eight characteristics of effectiveness are typically framed around objectives that donor governments and international agencies want to see integrated into projects, and not what is defined as important by people in need.[31]

The UN's annual consolidated appeal for humanitarian needs epitomizes this fuzzy purpose in an elaborate hydra-headed list of policy goals, priority groups, diverse activities, numbers of people in need and a price tag. It reads like a whole-of-society shopping list. It is not a system-wide strategy with a clear purpose and definition of success of what it is trying to achieve across its operations, with measurable objectives and a few common indicators of impact. Most humanitarian organizations work to a similarly vague framework in-house. This tends to start by noting global trends and priority needs and then enumerating individuals in need. It then commits to certain institutional improvements—like using more evidence, partnering better, digitalizing and becoming more diverse—before it sets targets for inputs, activities, outputs and the numbers of people to be 'reached' or 'served'. This input/output bias continues at project level, too, despite many bold efforts to aim more at outcomes and impact. It remains to be seen if 'big aid' efforts in new, people-centred accountability can change this.

Much time and money has been invested in programme evaluations to weigh the results of these commitments and their operational programmes. However, these seldom use rigorous impact evaluation methods that track objective cause and effect, and so they fail to report meaningfully on impact.[32] There is also a notorious custom in the humanitarian sector of getting insiders to evaluate agency performance, or critical friends who are more friendly than critical and hoping to get the next assignment, too. Agency staff often insist on reframing or censoring criticism, and they keep significant evaluations private and in-house. Objective whole-sector evaluations, like the Joint Evaluation of Emergency Assistance to Rwanda in 1996 or the Tsunami Evaluation Coalition in 2006, are sadly rare. Yet, both were game changers in important ways.

The last two decades of humanitarian elaboration and evaluation have culminated in literally hundreds of guides on humanitarian standards and good practice. These are usually extremely detailed, voluminous and a bit mind-numbing. Maybe it is just me, but to read them is it to enter into a parallel universe of utopian social modelling that it is hard to imagine being 'rolled out' in many places around the world. This technocratic detailing in big aid is no different to other spheres of modern life. Big business and big government have it, too. Today's business manager and social worker both have to be well versed in a hundred different types of knowledge, attitude, behaviour and skills. We are all being asked to be conscious and adept at so many different levels and in so many different fields. At times we seem to be unconsciously preparing a world in which only AI will be truly capable of taking everything into account and managing it successfully. We may soon hand over the majority of our detail to machines. Then, robot humanitarians may be able to remember and apply everything required in our standards and guidelines.

Until then, it seems important for humanitarians to remember and rediscover their main purpose and find a simpler way of going about their business and sharing the load with others. After a Baroque period of technical elaboration and a politically Romantic era of boldly proclaiming individual rights and protection, Western humanitarians now need to change again and work in a way that collaborates better and delivers more simply. This is essential if humanitarian aid is to rise to the challenge of a global climate emergency, and even big war, in the next ten years.

6

Changing Humanitarians

After more than a century of impressive progress and two decades of intense elaboration in humanitarian aid, a new generation of humanitarians must ready themselves for continuing civil wars and political violence, the climate emergency, possible big war, new pandemics and antibiotic resistance in the next ten years. These overlapping crises will make it essential for all people throughout the world to have access to a humanitarian system that can reach them on time with simple forms of relevant aid delivered through national humanitarian institutions close to them.

These three goals of global coverage, delivery by national institutions, and simple aid should drive international humanitarian strategy for the next ten years. Digitalization will help, and the current Western-funded international system is making important moves towards these goals. But it is still too narrow in its membership, too complicated in its ambitions and too internationalist in its way of working. New-generation humanitarians everywhere must design an aid system that is more broadly and fairly based across the world, and that extends in networks well beyond the core system funded mainly by Western governments. In this process, Western humanitarians should re-purpose to focus much more on enabling local and national humanitarian institutions, as originally envisaged by Dunant.

If global competition and decoupling between democratic and authoritarian powers turn explicitly to conflict, we can also expect many humanitarians to abandon neutrality in favour of forms of humanitarian solidarity and resistance. Like many of their predecessors, these humanitarians will take sides and deliver aid beyond the reach of neutral agencies.

Today's Western Club

The current network of UN agencies and NGOs, and the donor governments that invest in them, is routinely described as the 'international system' of humanitarian aid. This humanitarian system is certainly international, as the collective action of many states, but it is neither a global system nor a globally representative one. It is fundamentally a Western system. It is mostly designed and funded by liberal democratic states that are members of the Organisation of Economic Cooperation and Development (OECD), and its aid and policies are coordinated and evaluated by the Development Assistance Committee (DAC) of the OECD. The ICRC, International Federation and several large North American and European Red Cross and Red Crescent societies are heavily dependent on this system, too, while other large national societies, like Kizilay (Turkish Red Crescent), the Iranian Red Crescent, and the Red Cross Society of China stand apart to differing degrees.

The UN agencies, the Western parts of the Red Cross and Red Crescent Movement and the big international NGOs who co-drive the system all largely originated in Europe and North America. Most are still headquartered there and deeply imbued with Western democratic values. These organizations are increasingly diverse and are no longer staffed mainly by North Americans and Europeans. They have gathered international employees from many countries where they have operated and have promoted them through the ranks alongside citizens from their HQ countries with immigrant backgrounds. Humanitarians from the Pacific, Asia, Africa and Latin America, or with family backgrounds from these continents, now work at middle and senior levels of the system. But the system as a whole still works with a Western gaze.

Global powers like China, Russia and India stand back from this Western system and treat it with suspicion, as pervaded by liberal values and a threat to national sovereignty because of its tendency to 'interfere' in the internal affairs of crisis states. These major powers avoid financing it and certainly do not allow its many agencies and NGOs to respond en masse to emergencies within their borders. An expanding middle class across Asia, Africa and Latin America means that many national societies of the Red Cross and Red Crescent Movement are becoming financially independent of the West. Southeast Asian states have also pulled away from this humanitarian system in the last ten years, using its resources but controlling humanitarian policy in disasters in the ASEAN (Association of Southeast Asian Nations) region.[1] Most ASEAN states now insist on managing their own disasters, and increasingly their conflicts, without giving power away to humanitarian operations managed directly by Western NGOs and UN agencies. Many aid-recipient states in Africa and Asia, such as Sudan, Ethiopia, Syria, Afghanistan and Pakistan, have tolerated Western agencies but also actively resisted the system's tendency to dominate humanitarian action in their countries. Revealingly, Western humanitarians refer to such governments as 'assertive states' because they challenge and obstruct their work. This suggests they think 'submissive states' should be the norm when encountering Western aid agencies.

China's humanitarian policy will dictate conditions for many people suffering in war over the next ten years in the ever larger parts of the world within its growing sphere of influence. Although China is now actively funding and supporting UN agencies like the Food and Agricultural Organization (FAO), the World Food Programme (WFP), the World Health Organization (WHO) and even the UNHCR a little, it is certainly not investing in Western

NGOs or copying the West's humanitarian system with global NGOs from its own civil society. Instead, China is developing its traditional strategy for international humanitarian aid, which focuses on 'South–South cooperation' between developing country governments. This gives Chinese aid bilaterally to governments and businesses, and not to civil society organizations, and prioritizes infrastructure and health equipment.

Nor does Chinese aid follow the Western humanitarian tradition of direct individual care. Very few Chinese organizations are taking face-to-face responsibility for large caseloads of people in need beyond Chinese borders. At the moment, China is maintaining its core policy of 'humanitarian cooperation' with governments and not 'humanitarian action' for individuals.[2] Deeply embedded in Chinese humanitarian policy is the belief that if poor conflict-prone states follow China's path to development, then they can grow out of war and poverty. This core view sees humanitarian aid as merely satisfying a temporary need for food and health while China's main effort should focus on transferring its successful Chinese model of infrastructure-led development, prosperity and political order. In this, China today mirrors the West's early 2000s commitment to post-conflict state-building but from a different political angle. Perhaps the Chinese development model will be more successful. Perhaps it will not.

The Chinese government's main unit of humanitarian concern is likely to remain government capacity not individual need. But this could change. As China increasingly offers humanitarian support to countries along its Belt and Road Initiative in Asia, Africa and Latin America, it may well develop the Red Cross Society of China, and its military and state emergency services, as more individually focused humanitarian partners for states within its sphere of influence. In time, conflicts and disasters in China's 'backyard' and in countries strategic to its global power will test its important hallmark policy of 'non-interference'.

The strategic absence of China, Russia, India and important middle powers from the Western international humanitarian system shows that it is not an all-nations, all-ideologies world system based on a common approach to humanitarian need and response. The OECD system is a plurilateral club of Western states and big aid agencies working collectively across parts of the world where they have sufficient influence and interest to leverage their individually focused model of humanitarian action to reach, register and serve particular people in need.

The Western system meets regularly in a wide variety of policymaking groups in Western capitals, and in Geneva and New York, where they set policy for their expenditure and activities. Most important among these humanitarian policy forums are the Inter-Agency Standing Committee (IASC) and the Grand Bargain process. In neither forum are you likely to see representatives from China, Russia, India or the many African, Arab and Asian countries that receive Western humanitarian aid. The IASC describes itself as 'the highest-level humanitarian forum of the UN system' and dates back to 1991 when the USA and Europe were indisputably dominant in world affairs after the end of the Cold War. It brings together the chief executives of eighteen UN agencies and INGOs and is chaired by the UN's Emergency Relief Coordinator who is, traditionally, British. The Grand Bargain is a humanitarian reform process of the same grouping dating from 2016. It is driving a slow process of systemic reform to increase the efficiency and effectiveness of its humanitarian aid around a nine-point change agenda. These include greater transparency; more support and funds to local and national responders; a participation revolution that sees aid recipients deciding aid policy; joint needs assessments between agencies; and simpler reporting.

It is clearly wrong that the governments and NGOs of regions and countries affected by war and disaster have no real stake in the IASC or the Grand Bargain. This exclusion justifies criticisms of the imperial nature of the system. In meetings which routinely discuss countries in Africa, Asia and the Middle East, and set policies about them, representatives from these countries are seldom around the table. They are excluded and have no form of membership. Aid-recipient countries only get their chance to influence global humanitarian policy in the UN General Assembly in an annual resolution on humanitarian coordination every December, and when ECOSOC (Economic and Social Council of the United Nations) holds a three-day meeting on humanitarian affairs once a year in June. Otherwise, the rules and regulation of the humanitarian system stay firmly in the grip of the West European and Others Group (WEOG) at the UN because they largely pay for it and run it.

The exception to this rule is the UN Security Council, which, in reality, has become the highest forum of humanitarian decision-making this century. Since the 1990s, the Security Council has stepped into humanitarian policy to an extraordinary degree. After the Cold War, it began to take a concerted interest in the protection of civilians in the many civil wars that no longer had superpower patrons. Council consensus on these wars and on counter-terrorism priorities in the 'global war on terror' brought the humanitarian management of these conflicts and their resolution to the centre of Council business. The Council then began to design and back major new peacekeeping missions and humanitarian operations.

Many thousands of hours of Security Council time and many hundreds of pages of Council resolutions have been devoted to humanitarian policies of civilian protection, access, food, health, water, children, women and displaced people. This often causes the Russians to observe that the Security Council has become overly concerned with social work, which should be the business of the General Assembly. The lack of political consensus among the Permanent Five members in today's new era of global contest has made humanitarian discussions of conflict and humanitarian response in Afghanistan, Iraq, Sri Lanka, Syria, Yemen, Myanmar, Ethiopia and many other countries increasingly conflictual. Russia and China have repeatedly blocked Western humanitarian ambitions at the Council or have accommodated them to limited degrees. It seems likely that humanitarian policy will continue to be discussed, contested, compromised and approved in the Security Council, which will effectively remain the world's highest authority for war-related humanitarian policy.

A Colonial Approach

It is a distinctive feature of the Western system that the eighteen big players involved in the IASC retain tight control over its money and resources. Professor Antonio Donini has rightly described this group as a 'humanitarian oligopoly'. This oligopoly compares to regulatory capture by elite standard-setting groups in commercial sectors, like mining or oil and gas, that have fixed territorial interests abroad and which organize and lobby for their industry in line with their vested interests. In many wars, the big eighteen operate with a huge footprint. They employ thousands of people with humanitarian power held firmly by a highly paid 'expatocracy' that lives largely detached from wider society in privileged colonies of team houses, elite restaurants, big cars and bright flags. Operationally, these agencies routinely team up with parts of government and with national, sub-national and community-based organizations that have humanitarian goals or the capacity to deliver humanitarian aid. But most of these relationships are sub-contracting arrangements, with international agencies holding managerial, financial and policy power. Even if they are described rhetorically as partnerships and capacity-building, the working of the international system often communicates notions of inferiority to national humanitarians and is experienced by them as structurally racist.[3]

This international dominance over national and local humanitarian organizations and government departments has created a major policy dispute about the 'localization' of aid. Many states and many humanitarians in national and international organizations have long argued that much more humanitarian action should be locally led. The strapline of the World Humanitarian Summit in 2016 affirmed that humanitarian aid should be 'as local as possible and as international as necessary'. It is obviously not. The Grand Bargain commitment of the same year pledged to ensure that 25% of humanitarian finance is invested directly through national and local organizations. This has been a stunning failure, reaching only 2% in 2020.[4] The COVID crisis was a perfect opportunity to make these changes happen faster, but a fourth year of failure has increased criticisms that Western humanitarian aid is frequently imperial in style, colonial in its practices and racist in assumptions of its operational superiority.

The dominant business model of Western-funded humanitarian aid continues to be a top-down internationally driven approach. Most funding for official humanitarian aid is financed by Western governments directly to international organizations—UN agencies, international NGOs, the ICRC and other parts of the Red Cross and Red Crescent Movement. The humanitarian boom of the century so far has seen these organizations and many aid departments of Western governments grow into large transnational bureaucracies with many thousands of employees and multi-billion-dollar annual budgets. With money comes power. Western governments, and the international organizations they finance, control everyday humanitarian policymaking, needs assessments and aid allocation, although they are forced to operate within various constraints of operational space imposed by governments and armed groups on the ground.

The Right Balance of National and International Response

Finding the right balance between locally led aid and international 'big aid' is a pressing question in humanitarian policy today because the world needs to develop a far-reaching system of humanitarian response that is operationally effective, politically just and good value for money. The current aid platform does not cut it, because it is limited in its access, colonial in its practice, and centred in expensive transnational bureaucracies. Changing it inevitably requires greater locally led aid and better definition of the distinct value of internationalism in humanitarian response. Both sides of the localization policy dispute remain fixed but they must now work together pragmatically to imagine and build a better system. As such, it is important to explain the position of both sides.

Many humanitarians who lead or support national or local organizations champion locally led humanitarian aid.[5] Their arguments turn on operational effectiveness and political justice. They correctly argue that locally led organizations can be better connected to crisis-hit communities as part of society itself. This makes them faster and cheaper responders who are more in tune with community needs and there to stay. It is also true that 'national NGOs are always among those most present in dangerous areas'.[6] They also ground their call in political justice and sovereignty. Aid is for people in their countries and so should be put into their hands. The people affected, their own organizations and their leaders should be at the centre of decisions about aid's optimal allocation and should be accountable for its impact.

Localizers want national and local humanitarians to have more power and resources. They want to see them managing larger organizations that are built within the fabric of states and societies most threatened by wars and disasters. They would like to see more national and local humanitarian leaders around the table in the largely Western-dominated national, regional and global forums that set humanitarian policy and allocate aid funds. They want to reduce the power and numbers of the international humanitarian elite and rebalance it with a more representative elite of aid professionals from the societies where aid is invested and distributed. They want to work with international organizations as humanitarian equals and not as sub-contractors, and they want to see greater recognition for self-organizing aid beyond the UN-led system. This is often vital to people's survival but ignored and discounted by internationals, whose tunnel vision sees only their own imported system.

These fundamental moral and political arguments in favour of localization are about self-determination, equal rights, and citizenship.[7] The political right to self-determination is recognized in the first article of the UN Charter and in both International Covenants on human rights.[8] The charter insists that 'friendly relations among nations' should be based 'on respect for the principle of equal rights and the self-determination of peoples'. The International Covenants define this further as: 'All peoples have the right to self-determination. By virtue of that right they freely determine their political status and freely pursue their economic, social and cultural development.'⁹ A people and a nation have a right to humanitarian self-determination, which is a key part of 'internal' self-determination in a state. Instead, international aid is often operating a system of 'subjugation, domination and exploitation' of people's humanitarian self-organization, which are the three key markers of disrespecting and repressing self-determination.¹⁰

Humanitarian citizenship is a fundamental part of citizenship—a political agreement that citizens' lives are important to their government. This contract cannot be delivered from outside by internationals and must be made within the state. Indeed, the dominance of international aid agencies often disastrously diverts the process of humanitarian contract-making so that it emerges between a government and international organizations instead of a government and its people. This contract error delays the making of a real humanitarian contract for decades because international agency staff constantly enter government offices to argue for humanitarian rights while citizens are left outside.

Many people arguing for localization are demanding the right to play their part as citizens in building a humanitarian contract in their society and determining its norms, institutions and practices for themselves and their own country. To do this properly, they need to stop being the humanitarian subjects of an international aid emperor in

Geneva and New York who designs their aid response and liaises over their heads with their government on humanitarian matters. As citizens, they have the right to do this directly, even if it is dangerous and the result is ultimately uncertain, and they make mistakes. They should have the respect and support of the international system in this process, instead of experiencing domination and exclusion from their country's social contracts and institution-building. The West, like all parts of the world, has a long and vital tradition of 'citizen aid', but Western humanitarians are often blind to it or wary of it in other cultures.[11]

Ranged against the localizers is the much larger humanitarian establishment: the ministries of foreign affairs and aid departments of Western governments and the 'big aid' organizations they finance, like UN agencies, international NGOs and the ICRC. Most leaders of the Western aid establishment prefer the order of the current system. They have five main arguments for maintaining or tweaking the status quo. Internationals believe these arguments make international aid more 'necessary' than advocates of locally led aid are willing to admit.

First, they argue that national collapse makes it unrealistic to invest in local and national organizations, which are often destroyed by war. In such situations, it is difficult and even wrong to invest in the slow process of repairing a collapsed system at a time when people's right to life needs to be immediately prioritized. International emergency capacity is a more effective way to save lives and so honour the primary international responsibility to protect people from national failures. Second is the risk of political capture of national and local humanitarian organizations. Internationals worry that aid will be captured and diverted by politically biased, corrupt or anti-humanitarian cliques in the shrinking civic space of war. A third reason why internationals suspect localization is because they think its advocates are too purist in their definition of 'local'. Like Professor Kristina Roepstorff, they see local, national and international relationships as much more 'entangled' than localizers admit. Some local organizations are the creation of powerful members of the international diaspora who are neither local nor national in any meaningful way, and differences of class, religion and ethnic group within a country are often as significant as differences of nationality. Many international NGOs, such as CARE, World Vision, Oxfam or Caritas, have branches that are deeply national or local in some ways. Many aid agencies seem genuinely to be 'hybrids' that combine the local, national and international.[12]

The fourth reason is about guarding liberal values. Western governments have geopolitical concerns that localization would see aid money slipping away from the tight control of Western policy and accountants in an era of rising authoritarianism. Western aid is Western influence. Western values are under pressure today and need to remain as influential as possible, and aid is a way to do this. The current humanitarian order, with its operational scale and its ability to preserve and diffuse Western values in societies in crisis, proves the case for a predominantly internationalist system under their control. Socially, international organizations play a vital protective role for tens of thousands of people who might otherwise be targeted, arrested or conscripted in war. International organizations are a lifeboat for people who support Western values in a war. Many national employees in countries otherwise dominated by brutal militarism, negligent politicians, corrupt governments and a deeply misogynistic culture feel safe in an international organization where they are selected and promoted on merit, treated fairly, respected as women, and not put under political pressure to take sides or misuse and steal institutional funds. This perhaps partly explains why 52% of humanitarians surveyed in 2018 were satisfied with the level of participation and consultation of local actors.[13] Noisy 'localizers' may not represent everyone national and local.

Finally, there is the argument of global fairness. It is the responsibility of states and international organizations working together to agree global humanitarian norms and then to allocate global resources fairly when there are inevitably competing calls for humanitarian aid around the world. Local people need international humanitarian institutions who can allocate global money fairly and intervene impartially to deliver it as aid.

A Pragmatic and Creative Mix

A politically just and operationally creative balance between national and international humanitarians must be found fast, which gets the best out of national and international organizations and ends this energy-sapping policy dispute. The climate emergency, global COVID vaccination, and possible big war will demand both dimensions of humanitarian aid to be working powerfully and seamlessly together. Both sides need to be more pragmatic than ideological to make this happen.

Internationals need to back down on their exaggerations of necessity and lean in as real partners wanting to let go of power and redistribute resources. They have prudent reservations about political risk but they should not exaggerate these risks or the necessity of internationalism because of societal collapse. People in national organizations show extraordinary courage and political dexterity to remain impartial and often need support to do so. Furthermore, most war is not lived by civilians under constant bombardment and personal attack but in long-term conditions of displacement, poverty and everyday violations of their rights. Most aid flows into relatively stable humanitarian holding operations that support displaced people, basic services and routine human rights work to protect impoverished people in conditions of relative social order. These operations last for many years and involve repeatedly servicing the same communities, like the displaced in Syria, Iraq and South Sudan, the Rohingyas in Bangladesh, and displaced Nigerians in Maiduguri and wider Borno state. In truth, the typical humanitarian operation is much closer to a pro-poor development programme in a context of chronic poverty than it is to a fast-moving life-and-death disaster response. In these majority humanitarian settings, the necessity for international agency is low and the potential for local and national agency is very high.

Equally wrong is internationalists' misrepresentation of societal collapse and the weakness of local humanitarian order in emergencies. In reality, it is precisely in moments of collapse and crisis that new humanitarian activism, leaders and organizations are born.[14] The terrible war in Syria, for example, has birthed hundreds of new humanitarian organizations and hundreds of thousands of people engaged in mutual aid in their own neighbourhoods and across the lines of conflict. The Red Cross and Red Crescent Movement was born at Solferino, and all the big eighteen agencies and the norms and laws they have inspired were created in the conflict and crisis of their own societies last century. A time of crisis and societal collapse is the right time, and the ripe time, to be supporting emergent humanitarian movements in society and not overpowering them. We have seen this vividly around the world in the COVID pandemic, where new national organizations, innovative government aid and local mutual aid societies have rapidly emerged and flourished. Crisis is a creative moment and the time to invest in emergent humanitarian movements. It is not the time to pretend they are weak or do not exist. Sadly, the opposite too often happens. Professor Marie Berry's study of female power and women-led organizations, which emerged during the war and genocide in Rwanda and Bosnia, has some tragic conclusions on international aid's tendency to smother local humanitarian organizations and 'set back' national advances:

> Hot topics in aid rapidly shifted from one month to the next—varying from psychosocial trauma to microcredit—which weakened the efforts of high functioning grassroots organizations specializing in a single area. International experts displaced local experts; 'Western' training was deemed more credible even if practitioners had little knowledge of the cultural or social context... and deemed trauma counselling a top priority when many locals were more concerned about economic survival and establishing a daily routine.[15]

Internationals and national organizations need to get together to redefine their comparative advantage. Much of the 'localization debate' remains a war of words and lacks evidence about what works well in national and international organizations alike, and where they can find optimal 'complementarity'.[16] Many localizers have already urged internationalists to redesign their role and to become investors and partners who contribute finance, expertise, network and political cover to locally led groups and organizations.[17] This means reducing their own bureaucracies and their efforts to do everything directly, and skilling-up instead as originators and developers of national talent, and disseminators of successful humanitarian initiatives. International aid will still need some significant operational capacity that can step in or step alongside at moments of deep crisis. But an equally significant part of its culture and organization needs to change, to become more like foundations and asset managers who are investing in others for significant humanitarian returns. A new generation of international humanitarians should learn to become, and see themselves, as subtle spiders weaving a web of humanitarian networks, instead of heroic leaders commanding operations directly from on high. Finally, donors and international organizations alike must create simple accountability procedures and not tie government departments and national organizations in knots of ill-conceived and overly elaborate reporting.

For their part, champions of localization must not simply emphasize their rights but also lean into their duties. Article 29 of the Universal Declaration recognizes that 'everyone has duties to the community' in which they live. When national and local organizations rightly gain more power and money, they have a serious obligation to build effective and efficient organizations that can genuinely show how they are 'protecting life and health, and ensuring respect for human beings' in the war around them. Localizers must also show an element of pragmatism by recognizing the legitimacy of genuine 'hybrid' organizations that are a creative mix of national and international networks and traditions. Here, they should pay more heed to Edmund Burke than Maximilien Robespierre in their revolution by conserving what works well even if it is entangled and odd, and not insisting on an ideological ground zero from which to build every organization from scratch as local.

Humanitarian self-determination is a fundamental right and its success will be an essential foundation for effective aid in the huge challenges facing every society in the next ten years. Western donor governments and international aid organizations should recognize the principle of humanitarian self-determination as a necessity equal to their own duty to help, and so change the localization strapline. The current maxim, 'as local as possible and as international as necessary', puts the more powerful principle of 'necessity' on the side of international aid, and only a weaker 'possibility' of primacy on the side of locally led aid. This is wrong. The basic premise of humanitarian aid should be that it is 'nationally and locally led with international support'. International agencies cannot do it all and should not do it all. Local and national humanitarians who take up their right to build humanitarian organizations and institutions have a duty to do it well.

Humanitarian Cooperation

Shifting power to national and local organizations and building humanitarian institutions around the world requires a strategic shift in the Western system from humanitarian action to humanitarian cooperation. This means moving the centre of gravity from helping individuals in need to supporting organizations. Rebalancing towards a caseload of organizations from a caseload of victims will be traumatic for a humanitarian profession that finds its moral meaning in the face-to-face encounter with flesh-and-blood people. But it must be done. International organizations must step back from doing it all and being at the centre. Instead, humanitarian action must be replaced with humanitarian accompaniment, as supporting organizations, communities and societies—not direct intervention— becomes the primary means to humanitarian results.

On the ground, in their own sphere of influence, Western humanitarians must change their operational footprint from humanitarian action to humanitarian cooperation, and their caseload from individuals to organizations. In the last twenty years, Western humanitarianism has followed a highly individualistic model of humanitarian action with a heavy operational footprint. This has emphasized the direct agency of humanitarian organizations and the efforts of their frontline staff to secure access and encounter with suffering individuals. This expeditionary humanitarianism is all about individual international humanitarians 'going into' emergencies in foreign lands. Here, they work 'in the field' in self-contained teams with groups of individual victims, usually for a year at a time, while building large organizations that report back to their European or North American capitals. This is a story of humanitarian progress but also of a premier league of Western-funded international agencies intervening colonially, and getting bigger and bigger.

In contrast, humanitarian cooperation sees government aid departments and big aid agencies reducing their footprint and investing in the frontline footprint of regional, national and local aid organizations. In business terminology, international aid will need to shift a major part of its operations from a business to customer (B2C) model—in which an agency works as a retailer to serve individuals—to a business to business (B2B) model—in which an agency serves organizations to deliver those services. This works well already in several parts of the Red Cross and Red Crescent Movement and across many church-based aid networks. In war and climate disasters, there will be times and places where intense direct operations by international organizations are necessary, but in a cooperative humanitarian culture, this should be the exception and partnership should be the norm. International humanitarians should work with a simple localization rule: they should be enablers, not competitors, in the humanitarian sector of a crisis country. International humanitarians should never be ambitiously growing their own organizations in other people's countries but should be investing in new and existing locally led organizations in the society around them. Discernment will obviously be needed in this process—to choose which organizations to build so they support people and power that have genuine humanitarian intentions.

Humanitarian cooperation needs to be targeted at organizations large and small. It would be a mistake only to invest in making large national replicas of 'big aid' organizations, and investment must be spread widely across government institutions, social movements, businesses, NGOs and CBOs. Being good at 'small aid' investment will become as important as big or medium-sized aid. Working to support 'hyper-local' and 'survivor-based' groups without absorbing and distorting them in 'big aid' structures will be key. The Danish-based group L2GP rightly urges the culture of big agencies to change in order to stand aside from disrupting local initiatives and instead to distribute large funds in small parcels of micro-grants to communities leading their own survival and recovery.[18]

Cooperation between Big Systems

Humanitarian cooperation has geopolitical dimensions, too. Geopolitically, it means cooperation between different global systems of humanitarian response. Hardening spheres of political influence between competing Great Powers puts billions of people beyond the reach of the

Western-funded UN-led system. If international conflict or civil war emerges in the Indo-Pacific, across Russia and Central Asia, or within mainland China, the current international system and its Western operators will have minimal access to these geographies. New-generation humanitarians, therefore, need to develop a more realistic humanitarian multilateralism that recognizes different humanitarian spheres of influence and different humanitarian systems around the world. Humanitarian multilateralism should not be a struggle to ensure global access for the Western system.

Instead, humanitarian multilateralism in the 2020s should clarify how humanitarian aid is organized in each political sphere of influence as Chinese, Indian, Russian, ASEAN, African Union, American and Pacific humanitarian systems. Humanitarians in each of these spheres need to build cooperation between their systems to make sure each sphere can deliver for its people. All vulnerable people will be better served by humanitarian cooperation between mutually respecting and interconnected humanitarian systems than by systemic competition over a single system.

Non-neutral Humanitarians

If new-generation humanitarians need to accept a variety of humanitarian systems, they should also expect a variety of ethical approaches to humanitarian aid. Experience tells us that being humanitarian is universal but not uniform.

People can 'protect life and health, and ensure respect for humanity' while holding very different political commitments in a war. So far this century, most Western humanitarianism has held to a strict model of 'principled humanitarian action' that combines commitments to the principles of humanity and impartiality with the neutrality and independence of the Red Cross and Red Crescent Movement and its roots in the political neutrality of Switzerland, its founding state. This 'Swiss Model' of neutral and independent aid is one of Dunant's deepest legacies. Neutral humanitarianism insists on taking no side in war and political violence. It remains neutral in word and deed, and operationally autonomous in its humanitarian decisions. Achieving states' recognition for such humanitarian neutrality was Dunant's ambition at Solferino: to walk freely across the battlefield, caring for all in need, because humanitarians are trusted by all sides to be politically indifferent and engage only in saving life. This neutral approach has worked to great effect for many of Dunant's Red Cross and Red Crescent descendants. It has created a pragmatic humanitarian trust that sits above the politics of a conflict and has meant that many millions of people in history and today have benefited from protection and assistance because of neutral humanitarianism. From the 1990s onwards, UN agencies and INGO humanitarians have swung towards Dunant's Swiss Model and its neutral commitment to operate as trusted third parties in war, and it has worked for many of them, too, enabling their relief operations to spread widely across the geography of a conflict.

But neutral humanitarian aid has never been the only form of humanitarian aid in war, and nor should it be.[19] Before their pendulum swing towards Dunant's approach in the 1990s, many Western INGOs had not been neutral at all, and had saved many lives as a result. They had often been working in firm political solidarity with oppressed people living under apartheid, totalitarian dictatorships in Latin America and Southeast Asia, or rebel groups fighting for independence. They were determined and effective humanitarians who took sides. This tradition lives on, even if it has shrunk, and it has been on the rise again in non-neutral forms of humanitarianism among the Syrian opposition and among the humanitarian supporters of the many ethnic armed organizations in Myanmar and its wider civil resistance across the whole country today.

Non-neutral humanitarian aid as part of a resistance movement or the medical and social services of a party to conflict can still respect humanitarianism's deep principles of humanity and impartiality. Politically committed humanitarians can protect and save people, and they can do this for their enemies, too, whenever they come across them. This form of humanitarian aid has a long and ethically noble tradition. Importantly, it can help people in areas beyond the reach of neutral humanitarians whose geographical access, despite their neutrality, is often significantly restricted by warring parties, as is the case in the war between Tigray and Addis Ababa as I write in the summer of 2021. Humanitarian access by neutral agencies has been a constant problem this century. The rhetoric of 'principled humanitarians' gives the impression that neutral humanitarians are everywhere in a crisis and consistently effective. In fact, they are often very confined in their operational reach, either because of deliberate obstruction by warring parties or for fear for their own safety. The annual access report by ACAPS shows that 'crisis affected populations in more than 60 countries are not getting the humanitarian assistance they need because of access constraints'.[20] Most operational humanitarian diplomacy by principled agencies is devoted to a perpetual struggle for timely access to suffering civilians, with many agencies protesting that access is often in short supply when and where needs are at their height.

If neutral access is routinely imperfect and inadequate, then there is a moral imperative to try other forms of aid that are less constrained from seeking the approval and consensus of all sides. Aid organizations working in solidarity with government security forces, rebel groups or violently repressed citizens groups should be respected as humanitarians, and not stigmatized because they are not neutral. In many cases, such humanitarians are extremely effective in niche areas and may be cheaper than the large bureaucracies of their neutral cousins. With the return of the Taliban to power in Afghanistan, and the likelihood that it will gradually remove Western aid agencies, it will be interesting to see the quality of the non-neutral pro-Taliban humanitarian organizations that replace them and what they can achieve to protect people and reduce their suffering. It will be equally interesting to see how many principled agencies are able to stay and achieve significant reach.

The idea of political neutrality is not legally or semantically embedded in humanitarian aid, even if the last thirty years of international relations has tended to promote it as such. There are different ways to be humanitarian. Neutral humanitarians, like the ICRC and the Red Cross and Red Crescent Movement, can play an essential role with significant humanitarian effect. So, too, can non-neutral humanitarians, although often over a smaller surface of the conflict. People suffering in war usually need both, and, if the world moves into a new era of binary political commitments that set liberal democracy against illiberal authoritarianism, then we can expect many people's political convictions to render their neutrality impossible, and we will see a surge in non-neutral humanitarians around the world. Non-neutral humanitarians will rightly be saving lives and protecting people within social movements that are politically positioned as democratic, authoritarian, socialist, Islamist, or green.

Simple Aid

Humanitarians must be on their guard against unnecessarily complicated aid as they move into a new era where climate emergency and violence together put people under extreme pressure in many parts of the world. Investment in direct aid must be the future more than heavily intermediated and bureaucratized aid. The COVID crisis has proved the value and relative simplicity of direct aid. The domestic response of governments has put billions of dollars of small aid grants directly into the hands of families, businesses, community groups and arts organizations in their own societies. Humanitarians have also been adopting less intrusive forms of direct aid in recent years and must continue to expand them. Large, medium and small cash transfers and digital engagements should become the norm in wartime suffering and climate-related emergencies to support families, individuals and small businesses, and to maintain the large health, water, education and commercial institutions they rely on. Digital transfer and tracking of direct aid will be a huge advantage in these virtual systems, while it will also be essential to retain manual options for when the internet is unavailable because of flood, fire, dictators and warring parties. Physical aid in face-to-face healthcare, education and social work will still be vital for millions of people, but national institutions with less colonial baggage should be supported to lead these physical aid encounters.

A whole-society approach to aid will make it important to finance organizations as diverse as renewable energy stations, sewerage plants, businesses, widows' groups, refugee organizations or families with direct grants, and monitor their impact via big data. If direct aid increasingly takes off in wartime conditions, alongside investment in national humanitarian organizations, future humanitarian aid will operate without international humanitarian agencies as we know them today. Agencies will shrink and re-shape to become institution builders, joint policymakers and monitors of digitally delivered direct aid. This could be a good thing for the empowerment of national and local institutions, communities and families.

After twenty years of intense humanitarian elaboration, humanitarians should seek out simplicity. If wartime humanitarian aid is to reach farther in the worst of the climate crisis, new global health crises and possible big war, then it must become simpler to conceive, deliver and receive. Its current direction of travel is too complicated, too international, too bureaucratic and too expensive. National institutions and AI-based aid must be used to simplify procedure and transaction costs, as aid volume not agency aggrandizement becomes the goal. Systems of social protection should be used wherever possible to keep in touch with people and reach them digitally or directly as they inevitably move around or become trapped in places hit simultaneously by conflict, fire, extreme heat and flooding.

Dunant's great city of Geneva is not only home to international humanitarianism: it is also home to the international business of watchmaking. One Genevan watchmaker, Franck Muller, makes particularly flamboyant watches in a factory called Watchland in the charming countryside of Genthod, which looks over Lake Leman. The company's strapline is 'Master of Complications' and one of its most prestigious collections is called Grand Complications. These slogans haunted me during my time working as a humanitarian in Geneva. My experience suggests that many international humanitarians are too deeply absorbed in over-complicating their aid agencies and maintaining intricate bureaucracies which hire new global teams whenever a new humanitarian idea appears. I worry they do not spend enough time and intellectual effort putting available resources into the hands of struggling civilians. Obviously, a significant level of organization is required to achieve a significant level of effect. But it is my strong sense that today's large humanitarian bureaucracies need to trim down, re-purpose as enablers of national humanitarians, and work with much simpler ways of passing humanitarian aid to the people who need it.

If Dunant were to walk the war zones of today and work alongside humanitarians in the big international superagencies that dominate humanitarian response, I'm sure he would speak out against the horror of war today as he did in 1859. I am equally sure that he would lament the excessive complication of humanitarian bureaucracies and the waste of so much aid being channelled expensively through international intermediaries. As at Solferino, so again today: Dunant would see national humanitarians as the prime movers of humanitarian response and international organizations as supporting them wisely so that expertise and resources could be directly passed to national institutions and self-organizing groups in the middle of wars, and to the millions of ordinary people well able to decide how best to use it themselves without endless assessments and vetting.

The new generation of humanitarians now has a choice. They can continue to become the masters of their own complicated bureaucracies, that are trying to understand every angle of human identity and experience in war and respond to every kind of suffering individual with elaborate programming organized from enormous headquarters. Or, they can work to a simpler ambition. They can decide that global humanitarian aid is not a utopian project of perfection that should repair, adapt and reform every part of a person and the society around them. Freed from mastering everything, they can then focus on one big thing: sharing power and teaming better with local and national institutions to help hundreds of millions of people keep themselves alive as the agents of their own survival, and the change makers in their own society.

Epilogue

I finally visited Castiglione and walked some of the battlefield around Solferino in the late summer of 2021. COVID travel restrictions were lifted and I had already finished this book. But I was still determined to see the place where Dunant had become a humanitarian and launched his great Red Cross and Red Crescent Movement more than 160 years ago.

The landscape has been reclaimed from the violence of war by vineyards and buildings, but the horror Dunant witnessed remains memorialized in the huge ossuary of 7,000 skulls inside the Church of San Pietro in Solferino. The skulls were collected from the battlefield after the two great armies went their separate ways, by the same Italian villagers who tended to the wounded. Hundreds of skulls line the walls of the church, a sad prefiguration of similar memorials erected in Cambodia and Rwanda during my own lifetime, as well as the Holocaust memorials and hundreds of square miles of formal war graves and mass graves that stretch across Europe and the world. This book has shown how warfare is still making new skeletons and skulls in many parts of the world, while it creates catastrophe in people's lives and also reveals their remarkable resilience. The book has also shown that the killing rate in wars so far this century is considerably lower than last century. We need to keep it that way.

The world in 2022 is a very different one to Dunant's in 1862. But the twin challenges he instinctively recognized remain the same: to agree limits to our violence and to organize our compassion. Getting these two things right will save millions of lives over the rest of the twenty-first century. Both of Dunant's challenges are now dramatically renewed because of the new era of computerized warfare, Great Power contest, and climate crisis in which we live. The new multi-domain warfare I have described means that states must prioritize agreement on new rules for the conduct of war by AI-based warbots and for battles that may well be fought in our new global commons of outer space and cyber space. Dunant's ICRC is already energetically engaged in this process, and it is surely right for all states and citizens around the world to join in urgent ethical deliberation and law-making that prepares and protects humanity from computerized warfare and space combat as new normals in future wars.

The climate crisis means that wars will be fought in the midst of intense climate hazards, like extreme heat, fire and flood. People are already being displaced and impoverished by climate change, and their experience of future war will be made more terrible as a result. Living in mixed environments of war, fire, flood, extreme heat and new patterns of disease will be devastating for millions of people and will severely limit their options for surviving a war. I have also discussed how climate action itself may become a cause of war as people and states resort to violence in contests over mitigation and adaptation. This may well increase the extreme existential logic of armed conflicts in the decades to come. Here, too, the world needs urgent agreements on climate rights and climate action, so that burden-sharing and cooperation, rather than conflict, become the preferred choice for managing climate emergencies and disputes.

Dunant's second challenge—on how best to organize compassion—is also posed anew in our emerging digital world. Humanitarians have already started to do a great job of migrating aid and protection into digital space so that it reaches people in their virtual lives. This needs to continue wisely and at pace with significant investment, but without creating a blind spot towards the many people excluded from an online life.

I have also argued that the organization of global humanitarian aid must evolve fast in two directions to meet the challenge of warfare and Great Power contest during the climate emergency. Both directions require an emphasis on greater humanitarian cooperation at national and global levels.

First, humanitarian capability must develop much more nationally and locally in governments and citizen-based organizations. International organizations will not be able to do everything and must share humanitarian power and resources to build national humanitarian networks and institutions. This is the only way to achieve the reach and depth of humanitarian coverage that more frequent and bigger crises will demand. It is also politically just to end colonial forms of aid.

Second, Western humanitarians need to recognize a form of humanitarian multilateralism that builds a system of systems and that does not keep pushing for the Western system to be the single system. The principle of humanity is universal, not just liberal. States and people living in different political spheres governed by different systems of government and religion have humanitarian systems of their own. These must be recognized by everyone and supported in pursuit of a universal goal to 'protect life and health, and ensure respect for the human being' with a complete impartiality that works to help everyone everywhere.

Dunant was from the late nineteenth-century generation of humanitarians. I am from the 1980s generation. One of my great pleasures has always been to watch the next generation of humanitarians take up Dunant's great challenge to better limit our violence and improve humanitarian organizations. In the next ten years, a new generation of humanitarians all over the world will design and lead important humanitarian changes, and have other changes thrust upon them. Their progress will not be perfect, but I know they will be courageous and imaginative, and that they will help millions of people to stay alive.

Notes

INTRODUCTION

1. Henry Dunant, *A Memory of Solferino*, International Committee of the Red Cross, Geneva, 1986. Original edition published as *Un Souvenir de Solferino*, J. Henry Dunant, Jules-Guillaume Fick Publisher, Geneva, 1862.

2. Tammy Proctor, *Civilians in a World at War: 1914–1918*, New York University Press, New York, NY, 2010.

3. Hugo Slim, *Killing Civilians: Method, Madness and Morality in War*, Hurst, London, 2007, pp. 42–3.

4. Tanisha M. Fazal, 'Dead wrong? Battle deaths, military medicine and exaggerated reports of war's demise', *International Security*, vol. 39, no. 1 (2014), pp. 95–125.

5. Michael N. Barnett, *Empire of Humanity: A History of Humanitarianism*, Cornell University Press, Ithaca, NY, 2011.

6. John Fabian Witt, 'Two conceptions of suffering in war', in Austin Sarat (ed.), *Knowing the Suffering of Others*, University of Alabama Press, Tuscaloosa, AL, 2014, pp. 129–57.

1. WARFARE SO FAR THIS CENTURY

1. James D. Fearon and David D. Laitin, 'Ethnicity, insurgency and civil war', *American Political Science Review*, vol. 97, no. 1 (2003), pp. 75–90.

2. Harry Yorke, 'Nearly 60% of women in Armed Forces have faced bullying, harassment and discrimination', *Daily*

Telegraph, 25 July 2021, at https://www.telegraph.co.uk/news/2021/07/25/nearly-60pc-women-armed-forces-have-faced-bullying-harassment/

3.   Alexis Leanna Henshaw, *Why Women Rebel: Understanding Women's Participation in Armed Rebel Groups*, Routledge, Abingdon, UK and New York, NY, 2016.

4.   Asymmetric warfare is a twentieth-century term coined in Andrew Mack's 1975 article, 'Why big nations lose small wars', *World Politics*, vol. 27, no 2 (1975), pp. 175–200. The term 'peer-to-peer warfare' has re-emerged this century with the return to Great Power competition in twenty-first-century military doctrine.

5.   Christine Bell and Jan Pospisil, 'Navigating inclusion in transitions from conflict: The formalised political unsettlement', *Journal of International Development*, vol. 29, no. 5 (2017), Edinburgh School of Law Research Paper No. 2017/04, at https://papers.ssrn. com/sol3/ papers.cfm? abstract_id=2922470

6.   Erik Melander, Magnus Oberg and Jonathan Hall, 'Are "new wars" more atrocious? Battle severity, civilians killed and forced migration before and after the Cold War', *European Journal of International Relations*, vol. 15, no. 3 (2009), pp. 505–36.

7.   Anthony King, *Urban Warfare in the Twenty-first Century*, Polity, Cambridge, UK, 2021, pp. 2–4.

8.   Joel D. Rayburn and Frank K. Sobchack, *The US Army in the Iraq War. Volume 1: Invasion, Insurgency, Civil War. 2003–2006*, Strategic Studies Institute and US Army War College Press, 2019, p. 349, at https://digitalcommons.usmalibrary.org/cgi/viewcontent.cgi?article=1018&context=books

9.   *Encyclopedia Britannica* at https://www.britannica.com/event/Second-Battle-of-Fallujah

10. ACLED, Yemen Snapshots 2015–2019 at https://acleddata.com/2019/06/18/yemen-snapshots-2015-2019/

11. Hugo Slim, *Killing Civilians: Method, Madness and Morality in War*, Hurst, London, 2007, p. 57; Su-kyoung Hwang, *Korea's Grievous War*, University of Pennsylvania Press, Philadelphia, PA, 2016; Bruce Cumings, *The Korean War: A History*, Modern Library Inc. (Random House), New York, NY, 2011.

12. Robert E. Hamilton, Chris Miller and Aaron Stein (eds), *Russia's War in Syria: Assessing Russian Military Capabilities and Lessons Learned*, Foreign Policy Research Institute, Philadelphia, PA, 2020.

13. Clionadh Raleigh, 'Violence against civilians: A disaggregated analysis', *International Interactions*, vol. 38, no. 4 (2012), pp. 462–81.

14. Barbara F. Walter, 'The new new civil wars', *Annual Review of Political Science*, vol. 20, no. 1 (2017), pp. 469–86.

15. Thomas de Saint Maurice of the ICRC, 30 April 2021, on Twitter at https://twitter.com/thodsm/status/1388128268 834979843

16. Brian McQuinn, 'Armed group proliferation: Origins and consequences', *Armed Conflict Survey 2020*, vol. 6, no. 1 (2020), pp. 14–18.

17. ICRC, *Allies, Partners and Proxies: An Introduction to Support Relationships in Armed Conflict*, Geneva, 2021.

18. Luis de la Calle and Iganacio Sanchez-Cuenca, 'How armed groups fight: Territorial control and violent tactics', *Studies in Conflict and Terrorism*, vol. 38, no. 10 (2015), pp. 795–813.

19. Action on Armed Violence (2020), *Explosive Violence Monitor 2019: Initial Findings*, at https://aoav.org.uk/2020/explosive-violence-in-2019/

20. Urban Warfare Project Podcast hosted by John Spencer with Dr Charles Knight, 5 March 2021, at https://mwi.usma.edu/the-battle-of-marawi/

21. David Keen, *Useful Enemies: When Waging Wars is More Important than Winning Them*, Yale University Press, New Haven, CT, 2012.

22. Oliver Ramsbotham, *Transforming Violent Conflict: Radical Disagreement, Dialogue and Survival*, Routledge, Abingdon, UK, 2010.

23. Monica Duffy Toft, 'Religion, rationality and violence', in Jack Snyder (ed.), *Religion and International Relations Theory*, Columbia University Press, New York, NY, 2011, chapter 5.

24. Roger Mac Ginty, 'No war, no peace: Why so many peace processes fail to deliver peace', *International Politics*, vol. 47, no. 2 (2011), pp. 145–62.

25. Keith Krause, 'From armed conflict to political violence: Mapping and explaining conflict trends', *Daedalus*, vol. 145, no. 4 (2016), pp. 113–26.

26. Heidelberg Institute for International Conflict Research (2020), Conflict Barometer 2019, at https://hiik.de/conflict-barometer/current-version/?lang=en

27. Clionadh Raleigh, 'Global conflict and disorder patterns', paper presented at the Munich Security Conference, ACLED, 2020, at https://acleddata.com/2020/02/14/global-conflict-and-disorder-patterns-2020/

28. Paul Scharre, *Army of None: Autonomous Weapons and the Future of War*, Norton, New York, NY, 2018, p. 31.

29. Andrea Gilli and Mauro Gilli, 'Why China has not caught up yet: Military–technological superiority and the limits of imitation, reverse engineering and cyber espionage', *International Security*, vol. 43, no. 3 (2019), pp. 141–89.

30. C.J. Chivers, 'Small arms, big problems: The fallout of the global gun trade', *Foreign Affairs*, vol. 90, no. 1 (2011), pp. 110–21.

31. Margarita Konaev, 'With AI, we'll see faster flights, but longer wars', War on the Rocks, 29 October 2019.

32. Jacqueline Schneider, 'The capability/vulnerability paradox and military revolutions: Implications for computing, cyber

and the onset of war', *Journal of Strategic Studies*, vol. 42, no. 6 (2019), pp. 841–63.

33. ICRC, *Avoiding Civilian Harm in Cyber Operations During Armed Conflict*, Geneva, 2021, p. 33.

34. Ibid., p. 16.

35. Rob Johnson, 'Military strategy for hybrid warfare and coercion', in Janne Haaland Matlary and Rob Johnson (eds), *Military Strategy in the Twenty-first Century: The Challenge for NATO*, Hurst, London, 2018, chapter 12.

36. John Mueller, *The Remnants of War*, Cornell University Press, Ithaca, NY, 2013 (e-book).

37. Craig Jones, *The War Lawyers: The United States, Israel and Juridical Warfare*, Oxford University Press, Oxford, UK, 2021.

38. Craig Jones, 'Lawfare and the juridification of late modern warfare', *Progress in Human Geography*, vol. 40, no. 2 (2016), pp. 212–39.

39. David Kennedy, *Of War and Law*, Princeton University Press, Princeton, NJ, 2006.

40. Orde F. Kittrie, *Lawfare: Law as a Weapon of War*, Cambridge University Press, Cambridge, UK, 2016.

41. P.W. Singer and Emerson T. Brooking, *Like War: The Weaponization of Social Media*, Mariner Books, Boston, MA and New York, NY, 2018, pp. 5–6.

42. Andrew Hoskins, 'Media and compassion after digital war: Why digital media haven't transformed responses to human suffering in contemporary conflict', *International Review of the Red Cross*, vol. 102, no. 913 (2020), pp. 117–43.

2. NEXT-GENERATION WARFARE

1.   Department of Defense, *National Defense Strategy 2018 of the United States of America: Sharpening the American Military's Competitive Edge*, Washington, DC, 2018.

2. State Council of the People's Republic of China, *China's National Defense in the New Era*, Foreign Languages Press, Beijing, China, July 2019.

3. Dimitri Trenin, *Russia's National Security Strategy 2021: A Manifesto for a New Era*, at https://carnegie.ru/commentary/84893.

4. Rob Johnson, 'Military strategy and conventional war', in Janne Haaland Matlary and Rob Johnson (eds), *Military Strategy in the Twenty First Century: The Challenge for NATO*, Hurst, London, 2018, chapter 11.

5. Elizabeth Buchanan, 'Russia's 2021 National Security Strategy: Cool change forecasted for the Polar regions', RUSI, 14 July 2021, at https://rusi.org/explore-our-research/publications/commentary/russias-2021-national-security-strategy-cool-change-forecasted-polar-regions

6. Air Force General John Hyten, quoted in Connie Lee, 'Hyten: New warfighting concept to erase battlefield lines', *National Defense*, 9 September 2020.

7. Congressional Research Service, *Hypersonic Weapons: Background and Issues for Congress*, CRS Report, Washington, DC, updated 9 July 2021.

8. Daniel Deudney, *Dark Skies: Space Expansionism, Planetary Geopolitics and the Ends of Humanity*, Oxford University Press, New York, NY, 2020, chapter 5.

9. *Financial Times*, 1 April 2021.

10. Heloise Goodley, 'Supersoldiers: Pharmacological performance enhancement in the military', Interview, Chatham House, 9 June 2021, at https://www.chathamhouse.org/2021/06/supersoldiers-pharmacological-performance-enhancement-military

11. Amitai Etzione and Oren Etzione, 'Pros and cons of autonomous weapons systems', *Military Review*, May–June 2017.

12. Kenneth Payne, *I, Warbot: The Dawn of Artificially Intelligent Conflict*, Hurst, London, 2021, p. 19.

13. Thomas Rid, *Cyber War Will Not Take Place*, Hurst, London, 2013.

14. *I, Warbot*, op cit.

15. Ibid., p. 75.

16. David Silver interviewed on *Wired*, 23 December 2020, at https://www.wired.com/story/what-alphago-teach-how-peoplelearn/?mbid=social_twitter&utm_brand=wired&utm_campaign=falcon&utm_medium=social&utm_social-type=owned&utm_source=twitter

17. Peter Asaro, 'Algorithms of violence: Critical social perspectives on autonomous weapons', *Social Research*, vol. 86, no. 2 (2019), pp. 537–55.

18. More detailed discussion on these aspects of AI ethics in general can be found in the many contributions in Patrick Lin, Ryan Jenkins and Keith Abney (eds), *Robot Ethics 2.0: From Autonomous Cars to Artificial Intelligence*, Oxford University Press, Oxford, UK, 2020.

19. Wulf Loh and Janina Loh, 'Autonomy and responsibility in hybrid systems: The example of autonomous cars', *Robot Ethics 2.0*, op. cit., chapter 3.

20. ICRC, *Guidelines on the Protection of the Natural Environment in Armed Conflict*, Geneva, 25 September 2020.

21. Watson Institute, 2019, 'Pentagon fuel use, climate change and the costs of war', at https://watson.brown.edu/costsofwar/papers/ClimateChangeandCostofWar

22. Ben Barry, Douglas Barrie and Nick Childs, 'Dealing with hot air: UK defence and climate change', International Institute for Strategic Studies, Military Balance Blog, 16 April 2021, at https://www.iiss.org/blogs/military-balance/2021/04/uk-defence-climate-change

23. Mely Caballero-Anthony, *Negotiating Governance on Non-traditional Security in Southeast Asia and Beyond*, Columbia University Press, New York, NY, 2018.

24. Emiko Terazono, 'What growing avocados in Sicily tells us about climate change and the future of food', *Financial Times*, 25 July 2021.

25. Marshall Burke, Solomon M. Hsiang and Edward Miguel, 'Climate and conflict', *Annual Review of Economics*, vol. 7, no. 1 (2015), pp. 577–617.

3. CIVILIAN EXPERIENCE

1. Pioneers in casualty-counting include: the Uppsala Conflict Data Programme (UCDP), the Peace Research institute in Oslo (PRIO), Iraq Body Count, and the Armed Conflict Locations and Events Data Project (ACLED).

2. Taylor B. Seybolt, Jay D. Aronson and Baruch Fischoff (eds), *Counting Civilian Casualties: An Introduction to Recording and Estimating Nonmilitary Deaths in Conflict*, Oxford University Press, Oxford, UK, 2013.

3. Keith Krause, 'Bodies count: The politics and practices of war and violent death data', *Human Remains and Violence*, vol. 3, no. 1 (2017), p. 101.

4. See, for example, the United Nation's OCHA (Office for the Coordination of Humanitarian Affairs) Humanitarian Data Exchange at https://data.humdata.org/

5. Kelly M. Greenhill, 'Counting the cost: The politics of numbers in armed conflict', in Peter Andreas and Kelly M. Greenhill (eds), *Sex, Drugs and Body Counts: The Politics of Numbers in Global Crime and Conflict*, Cornell University Press, Ithaca, NY, 2010, chapter 6.

6. Syrian Observatory for Human Rights, 'Syrian Revolution 120 months on: 594,000 persons killed and millions of Syrians displaced and injured', 14 March 2021, at https://www.syriahr.com/en/209018/

7. Benjamin Thomas White, 'Talk of an "unprecedented" number of refugees is wrong—and dangerous', *The New Humanitarian*, 3 October 2019.

8. IDMC (Internal Displacement Monitoring Centre), 'The female face of displacement: 21 million women and girls uprooted by conflict and violence around the world', 5 March 2020, at https://www.internal-displacement.org/media-centres/the-female-face-of-displacement-21-million-women-and-girls-uprooted-by-conflict-and

9. For example, in the surge of migrants to the EU in 2015, 73% were male and mostly under 35 years old. See Pew Research Centre, 'Asylum Seeker Demography: Young and Male', 2 August 2016, at https://www.pewresearch.org/global/2016/08/02/4-asylum-seeker-demography-young-and-male/

10. Gudrun Ostby, Siri Aas Rustad and Andreas Foro Tollefsen, 'Children affected by armed conflict, 1990–2019', *Conflict Trends* 6, PRIO, Oslo, June 2020, p. 1.

11. Save the Children, *Stop the War on Children*, London, 2019, at https://www.savethechildren.org.uk/content/dam/gb/reports/stop_the_war_on_children_report_2019.pdf

12. CNN, 'More than 230 people fatally shot in shootings over the Fourth of July Weekend, 7 July 2021' at https://edition.cnn.com/2021/07/05/us/us-shootings-july-fourth-weekend/index.html

13. Clionadh Raleigh, 'Violence against civilians: A disaggregated analysis' *International Interactions*, vol. 38, no. 4 (2012), pp. 462–81.

14. Paul Wise, 'The epidemiologic challenge to the conduct of just war: Confronting indirect civilian casualties of war', *Daedalus*, vol. 146, no. 1 (Winter 2017), pp.139–54.

15. Alex de Waal, *Mass Starvation: The History and Future of Famine*, Polity, Cambridge, UK, 2019, p. 65, Table 4.4.

16. Les Roberts, Riyadh Lafta, Richard Garfield, Jamal Khudhairi and Gilbert Burnham, 'Mortality before and after the 2003 invasion of Iraq: Cluster sample survey', *The Lancet*, vol. 364, Issue 9448 (2004), pp. 1857–64.

17. Francesco Checchi et al., 'Estimates of crisis-attributable mortality in South Sudan, December 2013—April 2018: A

statistical analysis', London School of Hygiene and Tropical Medicine, London, September 2018.

18. *The Global Burden of Armed Violence: Every Body Counts*, Geneva Declaration, Cambridge University Press, Cambridge UK, 2015.

19. In Yemen, ACLED reports 12,000 violent civilian deaths by 2020 and UNHCR reports 4 million IDPs. In northeast Nigeria, the Nigerian Conflict Tracker reports 18,106 civilians killed in attacks between 2009 and 2021 (https://www.cfr.org/nigeria/nigeria-security-tracker/p29483) and UNHCR estimates 2.9m IDPs at 30 December 2020 (https://www.unhcr.org/uk/nigeria-emergency.html). Mozambique's figures are 3,100 civilians killed and 820,000 internally displaced, BBC, 6 August 2021 (https://www.bbc.co.uk/news/world-africa-58079510).

20. UNHCR in March 2021 at https://www.unhcr.org/uk/syria-emergency.html

21. World Bank, Brief, 10 July 2017, at https://www.worldbank.org/en/country/syria/brief/the-toll-of-war-economic-and-social-impact-analysis-esia-of-the-conflict-in-syria-key-facts

22. ICRC, 'Millions of young Syrians paid a heavy toll during "decade of loss"', 10 March 2021, at https://www.icrc.org/en/document/icrc-millions-young-syrians-paid-heavy-toll-during-decade-savage-loss

23. Physicians for Human Rights, March 2021, at https://syriamap.phr.org/#/en

24. Atlantic Council, *Breaking Aleppo*, February 2017, at https://www.publications.atlanticcouncil.org/breakingaleppo/

25. John Campbell, citing Nigeria Conflict Tracker, 2 February 2021, at https://www.cfr.org/nigeria/nigeria-security-tracker/p29483

26. Amnesty International, Press Release, 27 May 2020, at https://www.amnesty.org.uk/press-releases/nigeria-children-brutally-targeted-military-boko-haram-conflict-becoming-lost

27. UNICEF, 'More than 1,000 children in Northeastern Nigeria abducted by Boko Haram since 2013', Press Release, 13 April 2018, at https://www.unicef.org/wca/press-releases/more-1000-children-northeastern-nigeria-abducted-boko-haram-2013

28. Hilary Matfess, *Women and the War on Boko Haram: Wives, Weapons and Witnesses*, Zed Books, London, 2017, p. 89.

29. Campbell, op. cit., Nigeria Conflict Tracker.

30. UNHCR, 31 December 2020, at https://www.unhcr.org/uk/nigeria-emergency.html#:~:text=Over%203.2%20million%20people%20are,refugees%20in%20the%20four%20countries.

31. ICRC (2020), *When Rain Turns to Dust: Understanding and Responding to the Combined Impact of Armed Conflicts and the Climate and Environment Crisis on People's Lives*, at https://www.icrc.org/sites/default/files/topic/file_plus_list/rain_turns_to_dust_climate_change_conflict.pdf

32. 'Climate disasters "caused more internal displacement than war" in 2020', 20 May 2021, *The Guardian*, at https://www.theguardian.com/global-development/2021/may/20/climate-disasters-caused-more-internal-displacement-than-war-in-2020

33. Caron E. Gentry and Laura Sjoberg, *Beyond Mothers, Monsters, Whores: Thinking about Women's Violence in Global Politics*, Zed Books, London, 2015.

34. Thomas Plümper and Eric Neumayer, 'The unequal burden of war: The effect of armed conflict on the gender gap in life expectancy', *International Organization*, vol. 60, no. 3 (Summer 2006), pp. 723–54.

35. Dara Kay Cohen, *Rape During Civil War*, Cornell University Press, Ithaca, NY, 2016.

36. Gudrun Ostby et al., 'Organized violence and institutional child delivery: Micro-level evidence from sub-Saharan Africa, 1989–2014', *Demography*, vol. 55, no. 4 (2018), pp. 1295–1316.

37. Riyadh Lafta, Maha A. Al-Nuaimi and Gilbert Burnham, 'Injury and death during the ISIS occupation of Mosul and its liberation: Results from a 40-cluster household survey', *PLoS Medicine*, vol. 15, no. 5 (2018).

38. R. Charli Carpenter, *Innocent Women and Children: Gender, Norms and the Protection of Civilians*, Routledge, London & New York, 2020; and also R. Charli Carpenter, '"Women, children and other vulnerable groups": Gender, strategic frames and the protection of civilians as a transnational issue', *International Studies Quarterly*, vol. 49, no. 2 (2005), pp. 295–334.

39. Chris Dolan, 'Victims who are men', in Fionnualah Ní Aoláin, Naomi Cahn, Dina Francesca Haynes and Nahla Valji (eds), *The Oxford Handbook of Gender and Conflict*, Oxford University Press, Oxford, 2018, chapter 7.

40. Marie E. Berry, *War, Women and Power: From Violence to Mobilization in Rwanda and Bosnia-Herzegovina*, Cambridge University Press, Cambridge, UK, 2018.

41. *Pray the Devil Back to Hell*—watch online at https://www.idfa.nl/en/film/6674c862-4822-4ce6-a7df-974692a30a4e/pray-the-devil-back-to-hell?gclid=CjwKCAjw3pWDBhB3EiwAV1c5rF-BhYR4otsIJoHGQ5e0sk53-c3WAl2eGFU-NZSMdJ6d08-FyN2MVhoCsH4QAvD_BwE

42. Leymah Gbowee's Nobel Lecture on 10 November 2011, at https://www.nobelprize.org/prizes/peace/2011/gbowee/26169-leymah-gbowee-nobel-lecture-2011/

4. CIVILIANS AS SURVIVORS

1. Erin Baines and Emily Paddon, '"This is how we survived": Civilian agency and humanitarian protection', *Security Dialogue*, vol. 43, no. 3 (2012), pp. 195–212.

2. Studies of 'everyday resistance' go back to the seminal work on peasant resistance by James C. Scott, *Weapons of the Weak:*

Everyday Forms of Peasant Resistance, Yale University Press, New Haven, CT, 1987, and have been applied to twenty-first-century wars, especially by Oliver Kaplan, *Resisting War: How Communities Protect Themselves*, Cambridge University Press, Cambridge, UK, 2017.

3. Jo Boyden and Joanna de Berry (eds), *Children and Youth on the Frontline: Ethnography, Amed Conflict and Displacement*, Berghahn Books, New York, NY, 2004, p. xvii.

4. Erin Baines, *Buried in the Heart: Women, Complex Victimhood and the War in Northern Uganda*, Cambridge University Press, Cambridge, UK, 2018.

5. Claudia Seymour, 'Ambiguous agencies: Coping and survival in eastern Democratic Republic of Congo', *Children's Geographies*, vol. 10, no. 4 (2012), pp. 373–84. See also Seymour's arguments developed in full in *The Myth of International Protection: War and Survival in Congo*, California University Press, Oakland, CA, 2019.

6. C. Christine Fair and Bryan Shepherd, 'Who supports terrorism? Evidence from fourteen Muslim countries', *Studies in Conflict and Terrorism*, vol. 29, no. 1 (2006), pp. 51–74.

7. Jacob N. Shapiro and C. Christine Fair, 'Understanding support for Islamist militancy in Pakistan', *International Security*, vol. 34, no. 3 (2010), pp. 79–118.

8. Urban Warfare Project Podcast with John Spencer and Charles Knight, 3 May 2021, at https://mwi.usma.edu/the-battle-of-marawi/

9. Michael R. Tomz and Jessica L.P. Weeks, 'Human rights and public support for war', *Journal of Politics*, vol. 82, no. 1 (2019), pp. 182–94.

10. Oliver Kaplan, *Resisting War: How Communities Protect Themselves*, Cambridge University Press, Cambridge, UK, 2017; ICRC, *The Roots of Restraint in War, Geneva*, 2018.

11. Valerie M. Hudson and Hilary Matfess, 'In plain sight: The neglected linkage between brideprice and violent conflict', *International Security*, vol. 42, no. 1 (2017), pp. 7–40.

12. ICRC, *People On War Survey: Perspectives from 16 Countries*, 2016, at https://www.icrc.org/en/document/people-on-war

13. Janina Dill, Distinction, 'Necessity and proportionality: Afghan civilians' attitude to wartime harm', *Ethics and International Affairs*, vol. 33, no. 3 (2019), pp. 315–42.

14. Jonathan Chu, 'A clash of norms: How reciprocity and International Humanitarian Law affect American opinion on the treatment of POWs', *Journal of Conflict Resolution*, vol. 63, no. 5 (2019), pp. 1140–64; Scott D. Sagan and Benjamin A. Valentino, 'Not just a war theory: American public opinion on ethics in combat', *International Studies Quarterly*, vol. 62, no. 3 (2018), pp. 548–61.

15. Scott D. Sagan and Benjamin A. Valentino, 'Revisiting Hiroshima in Iran: What Americans really think about using nuclear weapons and killing non-combatants', *International Security*, vol. 42, no. 1 (2017), pp. 41–79.

16. Benjamin A. Valentino, 'Moral character or character of war: American public opinion on the targeting of civilians in times of war, *Daedalus*, vol. 145, no. 4 (2016), pp. 127–38.

17. Notably Jeff McMahan, Helen Frowe and other Just War revisionists.

18. Scott Sagan quoted by Clifton B. Parker, 8 August 2017, at https://news.stanford.edu/2017/08/08/americans-weigh-nuclear-war/

19. All figures, including percentages, from Simon Kemp, *Digital 2021: Global Overview Report*, DataReportal, 27 January 2021, at https://datareportal.com/reports/digital-2021-global-overview report?utm_source=Reports&utm_medium=PDF&utm_campaign=Digital_2021&utm_content=Dual_Report_Promo_Slide

20. Pathways for Prosperity Commission, *Digital Lives: Creating Meaningful Connections for the Next 3 Billion*, 2018, at https://pathwayscommission.bsg.ox.ac.uk/digital-lives-report

21. Kemp, op. cit., country reports.

22. Rune Saugmann, 'The civilian's visual security paradox: How open source intelligence practices create insecurity for civilians in warzones', *Intelligence and National Security*, vol. 34, no. 3 (2019), pp. 344–61.

23. ICRC, *Harmful Information—Misinformation, Disinformation and Hate Speech in Armed Conflict and Other Situations of Violence: ICRC Initial Findings and Perspectives on Adapting Protection Approaches*, 9 July 2021, at https://www.icrc.org/en/publication/4556-harmful-information-misinformation-disinformation-and-hate-speech-armed-conflict

24. Christopher Kuner and Massimo Marelli (eds), *Handbook on Data Protection in Humanitarian Action. Second Edition*, ICRC, Geneva, May 2020.

25. Zara Rahman, 'The UN's refugee data shame', *The New Humanitarian*, 21 June 2021, at https://www.thenewhumanitarian.org/opinion/2021/6/21/rohingya-data-protection-and-UN-betrayal

5. HUMANITARIAN PROGRESS

1. ALNAP (Active Learning Network for Accountability and Performance), *The State of the Humanitarian System Report*, London, 2018, sourcing Humanitarian Outcomes.

2. OCHA (United Nations Office for the Coordination of Humanitarian Affairs), *Global Humanitarian Overview 2021*, at https://gho.unocha.org/

3. Michael N. Barnett (ed.), *Paternalism Beyond Borders*, Cambridge University Press, Cambridge, UK, 2016.

4. Johannes Paulmann, 'Conjunctures in the history of humanitarian aid during the twentieth century', *Humanity*, vol. 4, no. 2 (Summer 2013), pp. 215–38.

5. Kenneth Whyte, *Hoover: An Extraordinary Life in Extraordinary Times*, Vintage, New York, NY, 2017; and Bruno

Cabanes, *The Great War and the Origins of Humanitarianism, 1918–1924*, Cambridge University Press, Cambridge, UK, 2014, pp. 189–247.

6. Claire Mulley, *The Woman Who Saved the Children*, Oneworld, UK, 2009, especially pp. 300–16.

7. Khatchig Mouradian, *The Resistance Network: The Armenian Genocide and Humanitarianism in Ottoman Syria, 1915–1918*, Michigan State University Press, East Lansing, MI, 2021.

8. Adam Roberts, 'Foundation myths in the laws of war: The 1863 Lieber Code, and the 1864 Geneva Convention', *Melbourne Journal of International Law*, vol. 20, no. 1 (2019), pp. 1–39.

9. Boyd van Dijk, Twitter thread for 70th anniversary of the Geneva Conventions in 1919 at https://twitter.com/boyd_vandijk/status/1160835867449155584; see also van Dijk's book, *Preparing for War*, Oxford University Press, Oxford, UK (forthcoming).

10. For these and other detailed statistics on the modern history of famine, see Alex de Waal, *Mass Starvation: The History and Future of Famine*, Polity, Cambridge, UK, 2019, pp. 60–7.

11. De Waal, op. cit., chapter 7.

12. Mouradian, op. cit.

13. IASC, *Leadership in Humanitarian Action: Handbook for the UN Resident and the Humanitarian Coordinator*, UNOCHA, New York, NY, 2021, p. 9.

14. See https://www.icrc.org/sites/default/files/wysiwyg/Activities/en-the_climate_environment_charter_for_humanitarian_organizations.pdf

15. See, for example, UNICEF's 58-page guidelines from 2020 at https://www.unicef.org/esa/media/7101/file/UNICEF-ESA-Intergrating-AAP-2020.pdf.pdf

16. Humanitarian Advisory Group, *Accountability to Affected People: Stuck in the Weeds*, Humanitarian Horizons, Practice Paper Series, 2021.

17. Protection Standards (2020) at https://www.icrc.org/en/publication/0999-professional-standards-protection-work-carried-out-humanitarian-and-human-rights

18. CaLP (Cash Learning Partnership), *State of the World's Cash Report*, 2020 at https://www.calpnetwork.org/resources/collections/state-of-the-worlds-cash-2020/

19. Patrick Meier, *Digital Humanitarians: How Big Data is Challenging the Face of Humanitarian Response*, CRC Press, Boca Raton, FL, 2015, p. 27.

20. HDX at https://data.humdata.org/

21. The German Red Cross and German government are leading much of the thinking and policy on anticipatory forecast-based aid—see https://www.anticipation-hub.org/

22. These ambitions are set out in the new *Operational Guidance: Data Responsibility in Humanitarian Action* from the Inter-Agency Standing Committee (IASC) in February 2021, at https://interagencystandingcommittee.org/operational-response/iasc-operational-guidance-data-responsibility-humanitarian-action

23. Rakesh Bharania and Mark Silverman, 'Protective by design: Safely delivering connectivity as aid', blog post, 8 July 2021, at https://blogs.icrc.org/law-and-policy/2021/07/08/protective-by-design-connectivity-as-aid/

24. The World Bank's FCV (Fragility, Conflict & Violence) work can be seen at https://www.worldbank.org/en/topic/fragilityconflictviolence/overview

25. Dorothea Hilhorst (2018). 'Classical humanitarianism and resilience humanitarianism: Making sense of two brands of humanitarian action', *Journal of International Humanitarian Action*, vol. 3, no. 1 (2018), pp. 1–12.

26. ICRC, *ICRC Strategy 2019-2022*, Geneva, September 2018.

27. OCHA, *New Way of Working*, Policy Development and Studies Branch, UNOCHA, 2017.

28. Stephen Devereux, Rachel Sabates-Wheeler, Mulugeta Tefera, Taylor Brown and Amdissa Teshome, *Ethiopia's Productive Safety Net Programme: 2008 Assessment Report*, Institute of Development Studies, Sussex, December 2008.

29. Ugo Gentilini et al., 'Social protection and jobs responses to COVID19: A real-time review of country measures', Living Paper Version 15, World Bank, 14 May 2021.

30. Asma Khaliq Awan, 'Linking humanitarian cash and social protection: Learning from the experience of eight National Societies', produced for Red Cross Red Crescent Movement by Cash Hub and Cash and Social Protection Working Group, December 2020, at https://cash-hub.org/wp-content/uploads/sites/3/2021/04/CashHub_LinkingHumanitarianCashandSP_v4-1.pdf

31. Shandiz Moslehi et al., 'Characteristics of an effective international humanitarian assistance: A systematic review', *Plos Currents*, 25 February 2016, vol. 8.

32. Jyotsna Puri et al., 'Can rigorous impact evaluation improve humanitarian assistance?', *Journal of Development Effectiveness*, vol. 9, no 2 (2017), pp. 519–42.

6. CHANGING HUMANITARIANS

1. Oscar A. Gomez, 'Localization or deglobalization: East Asia and the dismantling of liberal humanitarianism', *Third World Quarterly*, vol. 42, no. 6 (21 March 2021), pp. 1347–64.

2. State Council Information Office of the People's Republic of China, 'China's International Development Cooperation in the New Era', White Paper, Beijing, January 2021, at http://english.www.gov.cn/archive/whitepaper/202101/10/content_WS5ffa6bbbc6d0f72576943922.html.

3. Peace Direct, *Time to Decolonise Aid: Insights and Lessons from a Global Consultation*, London, 2021.

4.   IASC, 'More support and funding tools for local and national responders', at https://interagencystandingcommittee.org/more-support-and-funding-tools-for-local-and-national-responders

5.   See, for example, Charter4Change, NEAR Network, START Network and the International Federation of the Red Cross and Red Crescent Societies.

6.   GPPi and Humanitarian Outcomes, 'The effects of insecurity on humanitarian coverage: Secure access in volatile environments project', Briefing Note, November 2020, p. 2.

7.   Hugo Slim, 'Localization is self-determination', *Frontiers of Political Science*, 6 July 2021. Available at https://www.frontiersin.org/articles/10.3389/fpos.2021.708584/full

8.   UN Charter Article 1; Article 1 of the International Covenant on Civil and Political Rights, and Article 1 of the International Covenant on Social, Economic and Cultural Rights.

9.   Article 1, paragraph 1 of both International Covenants.

10. For a seminal discussion of self-determination and human rights, see Robert McCorquodale, 'Self-determination: A human rights approach', *The International and Comparative Law Quarterly*, vol. 43, no. 4 (October 1994), pp. 857–85.

11. Anne-Meike Fechter and Anke Schwittay, 'Citizen aid: Grassroots interventions in development and humanitarianism', *Third World Quarterly* (Special Issue), vol. 40, no. 10 (2019), pp. 1769–80.

12. Kristina Roepstorff, 'A call for critical reflection on the localisation agenda in humanitarian action', *Third World Quarterly*, vol. 41, no. 2 (2020), pp. 284–301.

13. ALNAP, *State of the Humanitarian System*, ALNAP, ODI, London, 2018.

14. Marie E. Berry, *War, Women and Power: From Violence to Mobilization in Rwanda and Bosnia-Herzegovina*, Cambridge University Press, Cambridge, UK, 2018.

15. Ibid., p. 193.

16. Veronique Barbelet, Gemma Davies, Josie Flint and Eleanor Davey, *Interrogating the Evidence Base on Humanitarian Localisation: A Literature Study*, Humanitarian Policy Group, ODI, London, 2021.

17. Many international and national organizations have already worked together to produce good partnership principles. For example, *Working Together: Oxfam's Partnership Principles*, Oxfam, Oxford 2012.

18. Justin Corbett, Nils Carstensen and Simone di Vicenz, 'Survivor- and community-led crisis response: Practical experience and learning', Network Paper, Humanitarian Practice Network, ODI, London, May 2021.

19. Hugo Slim, 'You don't have to be neutral to be a good humanitarian', *The New Humanitarian*, 27 August 2020.

20. ACAPS, *Humanitarian Access Overview*, July 2021, at https://www.acaps.org/special-report/humanitarian-access-overview-6

Acknowledgements

I am especially grateful to senior people in the Red Cross and Red Crescent Movement who saw value in commissioning an independent book on a topic close to their hearts, and enabled funding for its research and writing, even when the COVID pandemic meant we had to change plans and confine our ambition to a desk-based project. Helen Durham and Yves Daccord at the ICRC were early movers in the project. They were quickly followed by Alexander Matheou, Kimberly Brown, Eleanor Hevey and Maryann Horne at British Red Cross; Hanne Mathisen, Annette Bringedal Houge and Moa Nyamwathi Lonning at Norwegian Red Cross; and Christof Johnen at German Red Cross. Helen, Christof, Maryann and Moa kindly worked with me in an Advisory Group throughout the project.

Dapo Akande and Janina Dill generously welcomed me back to the University of Oxford to research and write again at the Institute of Ethics, Law and Armed Conflict (ELAC) in the Blavatnik School of Government. Here, I received ideas and encouragement from Ngaire Woods, Stefan Dercon, Ranil Dissanayake, Talita Dias, Federica

D'Alessandra, Tom Simpson, and many others. Giulia Biasibetti generously let me test some of my ideas on the Blavatnik blog. So, too, did Kilian Spandler and Kristina Roepstorff at *Frontiers in Political Science*, Wendy Fenton at the Humanitarian Practice Network, and Heba Aly at The New Humanitarian. Claire Hinton, Ed Archibald, Harri Lee and Valentina Barca patiently helped me to understand something about social protection. Eva Svoboda helpfully challenged some of my thinking on neutrality. As always, the Friars at Blackfriars in Oxford have inevitably influenced this book.

My two research assistants at the Blavatnik School, Nicholas Barker and Moshe Ben Hamo Yeger, were brilliant. I am greatly in their debt for pointing me to a wide range of scholarship and for introducing me to a new generation of scholars active in war studies since I last researched the subject in detail in the early 2000s. Thanks to them, I was particularly pleased to discover a large number of women scholars leading the way, from whom I learnt a lot. I have never understood numbers but have tried to use some statistics in this book. In the process, Keith Krause, Clionadh Raleigh and Catherine Lutz generously tried to explain various datasets to me. If I have misused or misinterpreted conflict statistics, it is because I remain hopelessly innumerate despite their efforts.

When lockdown reduced human contact so dramatically, I learnt a lot from people online, including a new generation of humanitarians and activists around the world whom I would not otherwise have met. Arbie Baguios, Sudhansu S Singh, Abi Watson, Tammam Aloudat, William Carter, Marie-Rose Romain Murphy, Degan Ali, Liana Ghukasyan, Aarathi Krishnan, Naomi Pendle, Jeff Crisp, Mark Cutts, and many others have helped me think on Twitter, on Zoom or in person. Vincent Bernard kindly advised me on my eventual visit to Castiglione and Solferino, places where I was meant to start my research but where I could only arrive when the book was all but finished. In both places, I was very warmly assisted by people from the Italian Red Cross, especially Francesco Rocca, Leda Mazzocchi, Sabrina Turrin, Riccardo Fera, Giuseppe Barrile and Elisa Zanola.

My children, Jessie and Solly, have been a humanitarian inspiration, as they have been throughout their lives. And it has been a special blessing to be locked down with Asma Awan while writing this book, someone who is a real humanitarian and not just a 'blah blah humanitarian' like me. *Solferino 21* is dedicated to Asma with much love and thanks.

Oxford, St Bartholomew's Day, 2021

Index

E Hevey